PROMENADE AND OTHER PLAYS

PROMENADE
AND OTHER PLAYS

by

Maria Irene Fornes

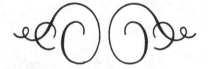

PAJ Publications
New York

Promenade and Other Plays is published by PAJ Publications, P.O. Box 532, Village Station, New York, NY 10014. Editor and Publisher of PAJ Publications: Bonnie Marranca

PAJ Publications is distributed to the trade by Consortium Book Sales and Distribution: www.cbsd.com

Library of Congress Cataloging in Publication Data
Promenade and Other Plays
Library of Congress Catalog Card No. 86-63187
ISBN: 1-55554-014-7
ISBN (13 digit): 9781555540142

Contents

Promenade

Promenade was first performed by the Judson Poets Theatre at Judson Memorial Church in New York on April 9, 1965. The music was composed by Al Carmines, and the play was directed by Lawrence Kornfeld, with musical direction by the composer, sets by Malcolm Spooner, costumes by the author and Ellen Levene, lighting by Kathy Lewis, and the following cast:

105:	*David Vaughn*
106:	*George Bartenieff*
Jailer:	*Michael Elias*
Mr. R:	*John Toland*
Mr. S:	*Christopher Jones*
Mr. T:	*Christopher Ross*
Miss I:	*Gretel Cummings*
Miss O:	*Crystal Field*
Miss U:	*Joan Fairlee*
Servant:	*Sheila Roy*
Waiter:	*Howard Roy*
Dishwasher:	*Frank Emerson*
Miss Cake:	*Florence Tarlow*
Mother:	*Jerri Banks*
Mayor:	*William Pardue*

CHARACTERS:

105
106
Jailer
Mr. R
Mr. S
Mr. T
Miss I
Miss O
Miss U
Servant
Waiter
Dishwasher
Miss Cake
Mother
Driver
Injured Man
Soldier I
Soldier II
Mayor

The roles of Waiter, Driver and Soldier I are to be played by one actor. So are the roles of Dishwasher, Injured Man and Soldier II.

Act One

SCENE 1

(The Cell. 105 and 106 dig and sing. The Jailer enters. He is out of breath. He sits and dries his forehead.)

105 & 106:
Dig, dig, dig
A hole to be free.
Dig a hole, dig a hole,
A hole to be free.
JAILER: It's been a hard day.
105 & 106:
Dig, dig, dig.
JAILER: Screwing all day.
105 & 106:
A hole to be free.
JAILER: Can't let the ladies visit the inmates unless they pay dues.
105 & 106:
Dig a hole, dig a hole,
A hole to be free.
JAILER: Oh, it's been a hard day. 34's wife, 48's daughter, 108's widow.
105 & 106:
Fly the coop.
Break the wall.
See the sun.

JAILER: Well, better get back to the ladies. Just came up for some air. . . . What are you two doing there?

105 & 106:

Dig a hole, dig a hole,

A hole to be free.

JAILER: Hm. You look like you're digging. Well, I better get back to the widow before she finds out her old man's dead.

105 & 106:

Unacquainted with evil we are.

This shelter protects us from wrong.

To discover the appearance of sin

We must go where the dog takes a leak.

JAILER: So long, boys . . . By the way, if you want to get visitors just let me know. (*The Jailer laughs loudly as he walks away.*) I can arrange it for you.

105 & 106:

The hole is dug.

Here we go.

(*105 and 106 disappear through the hole.*)

SCENE 2

(*The Banquet. There are Ladies and Gentlemen in evening clothes around the table. The Servant sweeps. The Waiter serves the Guests. 105 and 106 enter. They put on top hats and tails. They sit at the table and eat.*)

MR. R: Speech . . . speech . . .

MR. S: Let's play croquet . . .

MR. R: Speeches and music . . .

MR. T: Let's call Mr. Lipschitz . . .

MR. S: No speeches . . . No speeches . . .

MR. R: Let's have a song . . . (*105 and 106 clear their throats.*)

MISS O: Mr. T, was that you I saw on the corner of Fifth and Tenth?

MR. T: Perhaps.

MISS O: With Mrs. Schumann and her newly clipped poodle?

MR. T: Oh, no, it wasn't I. Friday night I was out of town.

MISS O: Ah! And how did you know it was Friday night I saw you on the corner of Fifth? (*They all laugh.*)

MR. T: Well, I must confess. The lady loves me. (*They all laugh.*)

MISS U: She shows good taste.

MR. R: Then, introduce us. She'll surely fall for me. (*The Ladies giggle. Mr. R writes in a notebook.*) Mrs. Schumann . . . lady of taste. . . . Bring dog biscuit. (*To Mr. T.*) What is her address?

MR. T: Tch-Tch.

MISS I: Oh, Mr. R, what perspicacity.

MISS O: Are you sure that's what you mean? (*Miss I looks a little embarrassed.*)

MR. S: Let's have a song. (*105 and 106 stand and get ready to sing.*)

MISS O: And who are these? Dear me. (*105 and 106 realize they have been indiscreet. They sit back at the table and pretend not to hear the others.*)

MISS I: They must be friends of Mr. S.

MISS U: My dear. You go right to the point . . .

MISS I: Mr. S does frequent rather unearthly places, doesn't he?

MR. T: What do you mean?

MISS I: I mean the lower depths.

MR. T: Oh, yes.

MR. S: If I am sometimes in the company of this and that, my dear, it's only because I like to study life . . . I am what you might call a student of life . . . This . . . and that.

MISS U: Oh, how incredibly personal you are, Mr. S. Have I not always said you have the artist in you?

MR. S: I am neither more than I seem to be, nor more than I am, and no less, also.

SERVANT: (*Mimicking in a low voice.*) And no less . . . also.

MR. R: Miss I . . .

MISS I: Yes?

MR. R: Last Saturday I waited for a certain lady who never arrived.

MISS I: You did?

MR. R: Yes.

MISS I: Oh, she couldn't come. She spent all afternoon walking up and down a certain street where a gentleman (*referring to Mr. T*) who shall remain nameless lives. She was hoping to have an accidental meeting . . . a sort of unexpected encounter with him. But he never left his house . . . nor did he enter it.

(*Miss O and Miss U giggle. The Servant is bored by the Ladies' and Gentlemen's repartee. Through the following speeches she pantomimes their gestures.*)

MR. T: He didn't, Madam . . . he didn't. He saw the lady from his window and she did indeed walk up and down his street. But he couldn't receive her . . . his heart was torn. You see, he received a letter from the one he loves (*referring to Miss U*) telling him his love was unrequited. He spent all afternoon sitting by his window plucking petals from flowers, and the answer always was . . . she loves me not.

MISS O: And who is this he speaks of?

MISS U: She is not free to love. Her heart belongs to he (*referring to Mr. S*) whose glance drives her to a frenzy, and whose mere presence brings color to her cheeks.

MR. S: The man who puts you in such a state has eyes only for O. Oh, Miss O.

MISS I: Oh! What tension! A name has been mentioned.

MISS U: And what have you to say to that, O?

MISS O: I regret I cannot speak since Mr. S has mentioned me by name. But do you wonder why O shuns you when you are so indiscreet? (*Taking a step toward R.*) And besides, she loves R.

(*R takes a step toward I. I takes a step toward T. T takes a step toward U. U takes a step toward S. S takes a step toward O. O takes a step toward R.*)

MISS U:
> You were there when I was not.
> I was there when you were not.
> Don't love me, sweetheart,
> Or I might stop loving you.

> Unrequited love,
> Unrequited love.

MISS O:
> Passionate lips are sweet.
> But oh, how much sweeter
> Are lips that refuse.
> Don't love me, sweetheart,
> Or I might stop loving you.

MISS I:
> Inviting lips,
> Alluring lips
> Which shape the word no
> No no no no no no.
> Don't love me, sweetheart,
> Or I might stop loving you.

MR. R:
> You know nothing of life,
> You know nothing of love
> Till you have tasted
> Of unrequited love.
> Don't love me, sweetheart,
> Or I might stop loving you.

ALL:
> Unrequited love,
> Unrequited love.
> There is no love
> Like unrequited love.

MISS I: Oh! We sang that well.

MR. R: He who scrubs the pot finds it most shiny.

MR. S: (*To Mr. R.*) And he who soils it, turns up his nose. Mr. R, you were flat.

MISS I: Touché!

MISS U: What a marvelous mind.

MR. S: Just frank.

SERVANT: (*Mimicking.*) Just frank. (*They all look at the Servant, shocked.*)

MISS I: Mr. S, it's up to you to think of a rejoinder.

MR. S: Dear me, I'm speechless. Wait! Listen to my answer.

> My frankness, my dear,
> My wit, my veneer,
> Are something you should revere.

LADIES: A rhyme! A rhyme!

MR. S:

> Instead, you just think it queer.
> Your unprosperous status
> Produces a dubious,
> Fallacious, and tedious
> Outlook on life.
> (*The Servant makes a face at him.*)
> You do not know what we're about
> We do not know what you're about
> Or care to know.
> (*The Servant lowers her head.*)
> It's sad your career
> Depends on our whim.
> On with your work, my dear,
> Or you'll get thin.
> You see, even if you're here,
> And we're also here,
> You are not near.
> Isn't that clear?

MISS U: Oh, Mr. S, how well you rhyme.

MR. S: Not difficult, dear. Just keep the ending of the word in mind . . . it will come.

MISS U: *Incendo, incendis, incendit, incendimus, incenditis, incendunt.*

MR. S: The ending, not the beginning.

MISS U: But Mr. S, how can one tell how a word will end?

MR. S: Foresight. (*The Waiter brings in a giant cake to the accompaniment of musical fanfare. The Dishwasher follows.*)

MR. T: Oh look! Look! Look! The cake is here.

MR. S: Oh look! Look! Look! It's time for dessert.

LADIES:
Don't eat it,
Don't eat it.
Wait until midnight.
GENTLEMEN:
Put it on the table,
Put it on the table.
MISS U: Phooey . . . It smells of garlic.
GENTLEMEN:
It's not to be eaten,
It's not to be eaten.

(Miss Cake steps out of the cake. They all applaud and cheer.)

LADIES:
Don't eat her,
Don't eat her.
Wait until midnight.
GENTLEMEN:
Put her on the table,
Put her on the table.
LADIES:
She's not to be eaten,
She's not to be eaten.
MISS I: What is she for?
DISHWASHER: To look at. (The Jailer's head appears through the door.)
MR. S: And to touch.
MR. R: Only to touch.
DISHWASHER: And to look at.
MISS I: May the ladies touch, too?
MR. R: No, not the ladies, only the gentlemen.
MISS O: I want to be naked too.
MR. R:
Only one,
Only one
Naked lady.
MISS O: (Taking off her dress.)
Two . . . two . . .
I want to be naked too.
MR. R:
Only one,
Only one
Naked lady.

All right,
Two naked ladies.
MISS O:
Thank you,
Thank you, sir.
GENTLEMEN:
Only two,
Only two
Naked ladies.
MISS I: (*Taking off her dress.*)
Three . . . three . . .
I want to be naked too.
GENTLEMEN:
Only two,
Only two
Naked ladies.
All right,
Three naked ladies.
MISS I:
Thank you,
Thank you, sir.
GENTLEMEN:
Only three,
Only three
Naked ladies.
MISS U: (*Taking off her dress.*)
Four . . . four . . .
I want to be naked too.
GENTLEMEN:
Only three,
Only three
Naked ladies.
All right,
Four naked ladies.
MISS U:
Thank you,
Thank you, sir.
ALL:
Only four,
Only four
Naked ladies.
Four . . . four . . .
Four naked ladies.

LADIES:
    Thank you,
    Thank you, sir.
MISS I: *Mademoiselle, comment vous appelez-vous?*
MISS CAKE: *Moi, je m'appelle La Rose de Shanghai.*
MISS U: *Est-ce que vous êtes française?*
MISS CAKE: *Pas au'jourd'hui.*
    Let the fruit ripen on the tree
    For if not the meat will harden.
    I'm the peach of the west.
    Chicken is he who does not love me.

    I come from a country named America
MR. R: You do?
MISS CAKE: I do.
    Chicken is he who does not love me;
    For there's more to the cake than the icing.
    A morsel I'm not, I'm a feast,
    And this not every man knows.
    Remember all the times
    You thought you got a bargain?
MISS U: I do.
MISS CAKE:
    And it cost you more than it was worth?
    MISS I: Aha!
    MISS CAKE:
    That's what we're here for,
    To learn one thing or another;
    For on art alone one cannot live.
    Chicken is he who does not love me.

    Tell me you adore me, and I'll let you go.
ALL: We adore you.
MISS CAKE:
    I'm the peach of the west, you know,
    And a bit of a rebel, just a bit.
    And chicken is he, chicken are you all.
    I'm not a morsel, I'm a feast,
    I'm not a morsel, I'm a feast,
    I'm not a morsel, I'm a feast.
MR. R: A toast . . . A toast . . .
MR. S: To the ladies . . . To the ladies . . . (*They all dance.*)
ALL:
    Only four,

Only four
Naked ladies.
Four . . . four . . .
Four naked ladies.
LADIES:
Thank you,
Thank you, sir.

(*The Jailer enters.*)

JAILER: Everybody's under arrest. (*105 and 106 freeze in an effort to conceal themselves.*)

MR. S: No, we're not under arrest, we're frolicking.

MISS I: Oh, what fun!

JAILER: Everybody's under arrest. I'm looking for two prisoners escaped from the penitentiary. And everybody's under arrest until I find them.

MR. T: Oh, silly man, don't you see we're having fun. Oh joy, joy, joy. (*The Ladies and Gentlemen start sitting around the table.*)

JAILER: (*Suspiciously.*) And why is everybody naked?

MR. S: Only the ladies are naked. The men are in full dress. (*The Jailer looks around.*)

JAILER: True . . . true . . . (*He goes after Miss U. Miss U takes a few little steps away from him.*)

MISS U: (*Pressing her nostrils with her fingers and striking a cherubic arabesque.*) Oh.

JAILER: Well, I may not smell of roses, but when there's a job to do, I do it. I'm looking for those prisoners and nothing can detract me from my search. (*Miss I walks past him. He follows her.*) I sense complicity here. (*Looking closely at her buttocks.*) Fingerprints perhaps . . . (*He touches her buttocks; Miss U slaps his hand. To Miss O:*) Madam, as an officer of the law I must conduct a search.

MISS O: Oh, stop bringing the street into our lives. You're common.

JAILER: (*To Miss Cake.*) Speaking of common, madam, I've seen you. You look familiar. (*Miss Cake hits the Jailer on the head. He crawls under the table.*)

MISS O: (*To Mr. R.*) Let us be irrational. (*Mr. R walks away. She addresses herself to 105 and 106.*) Let's you and me embrace. (*105 and 106 are not sure which one she means. They both start moving and bump against each other, bow to each other, offer the way to each other and so on. They finally reach her with open arms.*)

The moment has passed.

You have, perhaps, made me feel something,
But the moment has passed.
And what is done cannot be undone.
Once a moment passes, it never comes again.

I once had a man who loved me well.
His mouth was smaller than his eye.
But I loved him just the same.
Yes, I loved him just the same.

He said he would kill for me.
And I said, "like, for instance, whom?"
And he said, "like, for instance, you,
Like for instance you."

Sometimes it hurts more than others.
Sometimes it hurts less.
Sometimes it's just the same.
Sometimes it's really just the same.

But never mind that.
No, never mind that.
God gave understanding just to confuse us.
And it's always the same anyway.
It's always the same anyway.

If it's in your path to hurt me,
By all means, do.
But, I beg you, don't go out of your way
Don't go out of your way to do so.

You don't know what to make of me.
But I know what to make of you.
I have nothing to lose,
Or not much, anyway.
But never mind that.
God gave understanding just to confuse us,
And it's always the same anyway.

You have, perhaps, made me feel something.
But the moment has passed.
And what is done cannot be undone.
Once a moment passes, it never comes again.

(*Miss O joins the rest at the table.*)

MR. T: (*Offering Miss I a smelling potion.*) Have a little philter-philtre. (*Mr. R holds a bunch of grapes over Miss U's mouth while he eats a leg of turkey.*)

MISS U: Oh, how good these grapes are . . . To the left, Mr. R . . . a little to the left . . .

MISS I: Pass the syrup, Mr. S . . . You pour it. I like the way you pour . . .

profusely, Mr. S . . . let it flow. Ahhh.

(*The Jailer kisses Miss U's foot. Mr. R leans over and eats grapes from the same bunch as Miss I. The Servant and the Waiter wait on the guests. Mr. R and Mr. S offer grapes to Miss Cake. She looks at one and then the other.*)

MISS CAKE: I seem to be undecided. I'll take both, one from each. (*She opens her mouth. They each push the bottom grape of their bunches in her mouth with the tip of their fingers. She closes her mouth and they pull the bunch off.*)

MR. R & MR. S: Ahhh . . . (*They all begin to yawn and feel drowsy.*)

MISS I: Ahh, I feel a breeze. (*Mr. S blows in her direction.*)

MISS O: Sleep, sweet sleep.

MISS U: (*In a sleepy manner.*) I'd like another taste.

MISS I: Have you tasted the melon, Mr. T? It's sweet and ripe . . .

MR. T: Mommommmom . . . (*Mr. S burps. They start snoring. 105 and 106 survey the room.*)

105: Can you bear this bliss?

106: Yes!

105: The source of satisfaction is wealth. Isn't it?

106: It is. (*105 and 106 start stealing jewels from the Ladies and Gentlemen. The Jailer notices them and starts walking toward them stealthily. 105 and 106 move furtively around the room. The Jailer follows them.*)

106: (*Making a gallant gesture.*) Après vous.

JAILER: (*Repeating the gesture.*) Pas du tout.

106: (*Repeating the gesture.*) Je vous en prie.

JAILER: (*Repeating the gesture.*) Mon plaisir.

105 & 106: (*Repeating the gesture.*) Le nôtre.

JAILER, 105 & 106: (*Sing.*)

Après vous.
Après vous.
Pas du tout.
Je vous en prie.
Mon plaisir.
Le nôtre.
Permettez-moi.
Notre plaisir.
Le mien.
A votre service.
Au votre.
Au votre.
L'age avant la beauté.

(*The Servant kicks the Jailer out the door. 105 and 106 kiss her and resume stealing.*

They sing while they take the men's wallets and watches, the ladies' jewelry, the candlesticks, the silverware, the tablecloth and the chandelier. They put everything in their sacks.)

105:
    Can you bear this bliss?
106:
    No.
105:
    Can you bear this bliss?
106:
    Yes.
105 & 106:
    Eating is a blessing.
    Money is a joy.
    Drinking is a pleasure,
    And Riches a delight.
SERVANT:
    We've come to one conclusion
    That's readily discerned:
    A lot of satisfaction
    Does away with discontent.

    Doesn't it?
    A lot of satisfaction
    Produces happiness.
    And the source of satisfaction
    Is wealth.
    Isn't it?
    All that man possesses
    Displaces discontent.
SERVANT: What? What? What? What? What?
105 & 106:
    Diamonds and cakes,
    Macaroons and furs
    Dispel discontent.
    Chandeliers and wine,
    Porcelain and lace
    Efface discontent.
        (*106 takes a jewel from Miss Cake.*)
MISS CAKE: (*Taking it back.*) Oh no you don't.
105, 106 & SERVANT:
    Silverware and hats,
    Embroideries and salt,

Flower pots and yachts,
Cinnamon and bells,
And awnings,
And cushions,
And satins,
And rings,
And castles,
And crackers,
And things,
Things,
Things,
Things,
    (*105, 106 and the Servant exit as they continue singing.*)
Things,
Things . . .

(*The Ladies and Gentlemen begin to stir.*)

MISS O: Ah! We have been robbed!
MR. T: Where is my pearl stickpin?
MISS I: Oh, where, where, where?
MR. R: Where is my fur *porte-monnaie*?
MISS U: Where is my ruby tooth?
MR. S: Where is my monogram?
ALL: Where? Where? Where? Where? (*As they exit.*) Where? Where? Where?
    Where?

SCENE 3

(*The Street. 105, 106, and the Servant enter arm in arm doing a dance step.*)

105: Did you really like that party? (*They stop dancing.*)
106: Yes . . . I liked it.
105: I liked it too . . .
106: You did?
105: Yes . . .
106: (*To the Servant.*) Did you? (*She thinks a moment. They resume the dance step and circle the stage.*)
SERVANT: You know? (*They stop dancing.*)
106: What?
SERVANT: To discover what everyone has always known is not important.
106: No, it isn't. (*105 and 106 take a step as if to resume the dance.*)
SERVANT: However . . .

105: What?

SERVANT: I have just discovered what life is all about.

105: You have?

SERVANT: I have.

To walk down the street
With a mean look in my face,
A cigarette in my right hand
A toothpick in my left;
To alternate between the cigarette
And the toothpick,
Ah! That's life.

Yes, I have learned from life.
Every day I've learned some more.
Every blow has been of use.
Every joy has been a lesson.
Yes, I have learned from life.
What surprises me
Is that life
Has not learned from me.

Why? . . . Well . . . That would be hard to explain . . . If I could give you a kiss, perhaps you'd understand.

(*The Servant gives each a kiss.*)

You still don't understand? . . . No?

Well, then,
Because I'm placid as a cow,
As lucid as glass,
As frank as a bald head,
As faithful as a dog.

(*They start exiting doing the same dance step.*)

You see what I mean?

(*105 and 106 express doubt with their faces and nod. They exit. The Mother enters. She walks slowly across the stage. When she reaches mid-stage she turns to the audience.*)

MOTHER: Have you seen my babies? (*Pause.*) No? . . . All right.

(*She exits. There is the sound of a car, brakes, and a crash. The Injured Man is hurled on stage. The car is heard starting and taking off at high speed. 105, 106 and the Servant enter. They look the Injured Man over. They pull the top of their sack open and give it to the Servant to hold. 106 takes the Injured Man's wallet, watch, ring, shoes, and jacket, and passes them to 105 who puts them in the sack. They start tiptoeing*) *away.)*

INJURED MAN: Ohh . . . (*105, 106 and the Servant stop short.*) Ohhh . . . ohh . . .
105: (*Still without moving.*) What was that?
INJURED MAN: Ohhh . . . (*105, 106 and the Servant tiptoe to the Injured Man. 105 picks up the Injured Man's arm.*) Ohhh . . . (*105 drops the arm. There is a short pause. He picks up the other arm.*) Ohhh . . . (*105 drops the arm.*) Ohhh . . .

105: He aches. (*They look at each other. They look at the Injured Man. The Driver enters.*)
DRIVER: I came back.
INJURED MAN: Ohh. Ohh.
DRIVER: To the scene of the crime.
INJURED MAN: Ohh. Ohh.
DRIVER: I'm a hit-and-run driver.
INJURED MAN: Ohh. Ohh.
DRIVER: I'll kill myself if you die.
INJURED MAN: Ohh. Ohh. I'm cold. (*The Jailer enters.*)
JAILER: Have you seen two prisoners escaped from the penitentiary? One tall. The other just a little taller? (*105 and 106 lie as injured.*) They wear prisoners' uniforms with the number 105 and 106 on the front and on the back of their jackets. (*105 and 106 take off their jackets and put them on the Injured Man. The number 105 is visible on his chest and 106 on his back.*)
INJURED MAN:
  Thank you,
  Thank you.
  You're so nice,
  You're so nice.
  Thank you,
  Thank you.
  You're so nice,
  You're so nice.
  Thank you,
  Oh, thank you.
JAILER: (*Pointing to the Injured Man.*) That's one of them! Get up, 105. (*The Jailer hits the Injured Man on the stomach. The Injured Man bends over. The number 106 is visible on his back.*) There's the other. Get up, 106. That's them all right. Get up.
DRIVER: Leave him alone. You're kicking the injured man.
JAILER: What do you mean? That's 105 and 106.
DRIVER: Does that look like two people to you? That's the injured man. (*105 and 106 begin to shiver.*)
INJURED MAN: My friends are cold, too. Someone must have stolen their

clothes.

DRIVER: I'll take the clothes off my back to give to your friends. If you die I'll kill myself. (*The Driver gives his jacket and vest to 105 and 106. He shivers.*) Now I'm cold.

INJURED MAN: (*Giving one of the jackets to the Driver.*) I have enough for two.

JAILER: Which reminds me of this little woman I used to have. She used to take her clothes off all the time. That was the only thing I liked about her . . . hey! There you are, 105 and 106. (*Taking the Driver and the Injured Man by the collar.*) Don't tell me you're just one. I see you plain as day. One and two. I can count. Don't tell me I can't count. (*He exits with the Driver and the Injured Man.*)

SERVANT:
Neither probe nor ignore
That the clothes make the man.
Isn't it true that costumes
Change the course of life?

Who can marry a gigolo?
Can you?
Can you?
I can't.

Who can love a businessman?
Can you?
Can you?
I can't.

Who can pity a cop?
Who can reason with a clown?
Who can dance with a priest?
Can you?
Can you?
I can't.

105, 106 & SERVANT:
You see, a costume
Can change your life.
Be one and all.
Be each and all.
Transvest,
Impersonate,
'Cause costumes
Change the course
Of life.

(*The Jailer re-enters, carrying the prisoners' jackets by the collar.*)

JAILER: I'm taking these two prisoners back to jail. (*He shrugs his shoulders and exits.*)

105, 106 & SERVANT:
Who can argue with a jailer?
Can you?
Can you?
I can't.

Be one and all.
Be each and all.
Transvest,
Impersonate,
'Cause costumes
Change the course
Of life.

(*They exit.*)

SCENE 4

(*The Park. 105 and 106 sit on a bench. They each knit one end of a single scarf. The Servant sits between them. The Mother enters.*)

MOTHER: I've lost my babies. I've been looking for them for years and I can't find them. Have you seen them?

106: No.

MOTHER: You haven't seen my babies, have you?

SERVANT: No.

MOTHER: They aren't very pretty, but they have beautiful eyes. I lost my babies right here. Have you seen them?

105 & 106: No.

MOTHER:
Have you seen my babies?
I've been looking for them for years,
And I can't find them.

Have you seen them?
Have you seen them?
Have you seen them?

Have you seen two little angels?
Have you? With skin soft like feathers
In diapers still.

Have you seen them?
Have you seen them?

Have you seen them?

Have you seen those sweet angels?
Have you seen them . . .

    (*The Mother looks closely at 105 and 106.*)

No . . . My babies were pretty. These are not my babies. (*She looks again.*)
No. These are big, ugly and old. Mine were this big. (*She indicates the size of
an infant.*) And pretty . . . Bye.

105 & 106: Bye. (*The Mother exits.*)

106: Hmm. Big, ugly and old . . .

105: Well, we could be younger. (*The Mother re-enters and watches 105 and 106
from behind the bushes.*)

106: True.

105: We could be prettier.

106: Not true.

105: We could be smaller.

106: Don't want to be.

105 & 106:

    It's to age
    That we owe
    What we are.

    In fact we're grateful
    For the passing of time.
    It's only fitting
    We should be grateful
    For the passing of time.
    'Cause
    Without growth
    We'd not be
    What we are.

MOTHER: What are you? (*They pose for her. They point to themselves from head to
toe. They do a turn. They do a tap step.*)

105 & 106:

    We are
    All that we are.
    From head to toe.

    Once it's thoroughly thought through
    We should realize
    It's only appropriate
    We should be attracted
    To the passing of time,
    Attracted to the passing of time.

'Cause it's to age
That we owe what we are,
And without it
We'd not be
What we are.

MOTHER: It's distressing to get old.

106: Well, you are bound to get older . . .

105: If you're going to be alive.

(*The Ladies and Gentlemen walk in, led by Mr. S, who scans the floor for footprints. They walk by 105, 106 and the Servant without noticing them.*)

MR. S: They went this way. Follow me. I took a course in trails, tracks and clues. (*He discovers Miss U's foot.*) Oh, what pretty feet you have, Miss U.

MISS U: I do?

MR. T: Feet? Where? Oh . . .

MR. S: Dainty.

MR. T: Hm. Delicious. (*Lifting her skirt.*) Let's see your ankle, Miss U. Oh, it's pretty.

MISS U: Mr. R, wouldn't you like to admire my feet? Each toe has a personality all its own.

MR. R: Oh, I've seen them.

MISS U: You cad. (*To Mr. S and Mr. T.*) Who am I?

MR. S & MR. T: The queen!

MISS U: And what are my virtues? (*Mr. S and Mr. T lift her up on their shoulders.*)

MR. S & MR. T: You are flighty! You are fickle! And you are wicked!

MISS U: That's right. (*They put her down. Miss U walks to Mr. R. He turns his back to her.*)
You rascal.

Capricious as I am, and fickle,
In spite of my renowned restlessness,
In spite of my noted changeability;
My versatility, my spirit of adventure,
One day because of your winning ways.
I gave you all I had.
And you in your typical fashion,
Conceited, flippant, and complacent,
Just threw it all away,
Just threw it all away.
You heel! You cad!
You treated me the way I treated others.
You scoundrel!
How dare you bring shame to my life? Shame . . . shame.

One day, because of your amorous claims,
I learned that pleasure
Does not need fabrication;
That true love catches you by surprise.
But you, confirmed egotist,
You were just playing games.

You insisted on re-enacting
A moment from your past;
Either a moment that you lived
Or a moment that you imagined.
You heel! You were just playing games. Shame . . . shame . . .

I am conceited, flippant and deceitful,
And I am flighty, frivolous, and vain.
And you, scoundrel,
You treated me the way I treated others.
Just who do you think you are?

In spite of my reputation
As a lady without heart
I gave my heart to you.
You heel . . .
And here I am.
I've lost my heart to you.

Unaccustomed as I am
To asking a man for his favor,
I'm asking you,
Come . . . come . . . come . . .
I'm helpless without you.

(*Mr. R walks to Miss U. They kiss. Immediately after, Mr. R touches Miss I's face and blows her a kiss. Miss U punches Mr. R in the stomach. Mr. R falls. Mr. T and Mr. S carry him off followed by Miss O, Miss I, Miss U, and the Mother.*)

SERVANT: Ahhhh. Riches made them dumb.
105: Who?
SERVANT: All of them. Mr. R, Mr. S, Mr. T, Miss I, Miss O, Miss U.
105: Really?
SERVANT: Yes, money made them dumb.
106: Did it? How dumb.
SERVANT: Very dumb. Money makes you dumb.
106: Naw . . .
SERVANT: Yes! . . . I'll show you. (*She puts on a bracelet, a necklace and a brooch. She imitates the speech of the Ladies and Gentlemen.*) If someone scrubs the pot.

Perhaps it will get shiny. I'm neither this, nor that. Only exactly what I think I am. That is, if you think I'm frank, frank, frank. (*She reaches for more jewels. 105 and 106 begin to dress her. They drape a lace tablecloth around her, hang the silverware around her waist and put the rest of the jewelry on her. At the end of the song they put the chandelier on her head as a crown.*)
Is it time yet to be naked?
Oh no no no no no, oh no.
It might be a little indiscreet
To take off my clothes before three.
Aah . . . aah . . . aah . . .

It is now time to get dressed.
Dress, dress, dress, dress, dress me.
It is time to put on my clothes.
Aah . . . aah . . . aah . . .

In my life I've made some errors.
Errors one and two and three,
Four, five, six,
Seven, eight, nine, ten.
Wonderful errors. Marvelous errors.
From a to z.

I used to be an ordinary girl
With a delicate soul.
Now I'm just ordinary.
Where did my soul go?
Aah . . . aah . . . aah
Where did it go?
Where did my soul go?

Someone has mentioned my name.
But who is it he speaks of?
You see I'm neither this nor that,
Neither this nor that.
And I'm not free to love.

Someone has mentioned my name
But I'm neither this nor that.
And I've forgotten who I am,
I've forgotten who I am.
But I can, I can, I can rhyme,
Yme,* yme, yme, yme, yme,
I can, I can, I can rhyme,
Yme, yme, yme, yme, yme.

---

*Pronounced ime.

Why have you not crowned me yet.
I'm neither this nor that
But I can rhyme.
I can rhyme
Yme, yme, yme, yme.

(*They crown her.*)

I can rhyme
Yme, yme, yme, yme, yme.
You see what I mean?
105: Not really. (*106 shakes his head.*)
SERVANT: (*In an attempt to convince them.*)
Yme yme yme yme yme yme
Rhyme.

It's also bad for your health. (*She sneezes.*)
106: Are you rich, dear? You seem to have a cold.
SERVANT: I used to be poor. Very, very poor. But now, I'm very, very, very
rich. (*She sneezes.*)
105: You are?
SERVANT: Yes.
106: Watch out you don't lose your brains. Remember, riches make you dumb.
Ho ho ho.
105: And you are even beginning to imagine things. Ho ho.
106:
Riches make you dumb.
105:
Yme, yme, yme, rhyme.
SERVANT:
I can rhyme.

(*105 places the sack on the floor next to the Servant, while 106 picks her up and stands
her on the sack. Now she is part of their loot. The Jailer watches from a corner. They
pull the sack over the Servant's head, carry her on their shoulders and exit.*)

Act Two

SCENE 1

(*The Battlefield. There is the sound of bombs. The lights flash on and off. Soldiers I and II lie on the floor. Their heads, arms, and torsos are wrapped in bandages. 105 and 106 run across the stage. They still carry the Servant. The Jailer follows them. He stops when he sees the Soldiers.*)

JAILER: There you are, 105 and 106, you're digging. Your disguise does not deceive me. I'd recognize you miles away. I'm a smart man and your tricks are puerile. (*Bomb.*) I think I'll watch from afar. This time they're playing with dynamite and a man can get hurt with that. (*Bomb. He exits.*)

SOLDIER I: John . . .

SOLDIER II: What?

SOLDIER I: Did you get drafted?

SOLDIER II: Drafted!

SOLDIER I: Did you volunteer?

SOLDIER II: For what?

SOLDIER I: To get the bombs dropped on you.

SOLDIER II: No, I didn't.

SOLDIER I: How did they get you?

SOLDIER II: I was going home from work when someone said: "Hey, soldier!" and I made the mistake to look.

SOLDIER I: You volunteered then.

SOLDIER II: Why?

SOLDIER I: Because you looked.

SOLDIER II: Gosh! I shouldn't have looked.

SOLDIER I: Well, they get you anyway, whether you look or not.

SOLDIER II: How did they get you?

SOLDIER I: I got drafted. When the man said "Hey, soldier," I kept walking. But he hit me on the head, told me to drop my pants, spread my cheeks, threw me on a barber chair, and here I am. . . . They didn't even let me face the mirror.

SOLDIER II: That's tough.

SOLDIER I: John, we used to have a good time, didn't we?

SOLDIER II: Yes, remember the time we got in trouble by the fountain?

SOLDIER I: *You* got in trouble.

SOLDIER II: I was a little drunk. And there was a cop standing in the corner. And I said to him "Hey, flatfoot." . . . Ha ha ha ha ha. . . . It was a nice evening.

SOLDIER I: John . . .

SOLDIER II: What?

SOLDIER I: Do you think we're going to win the war?

SOLDIER II: We might.

SOLDIER I: How can we? We don't even have guns.

SOLDIER II: Only bandages.

SOLDIER I: What can we do with bandages?

SOLDIER II: Just wait till we get hit, I guess. (*A bomb falls. At the same time 105 and 106 are hurled on stage. Their heads and torsos are wrapped in bandages. Soldiers I and II fall to the ground. Another bomb falls. 105 and 106 huddle up to the soldiers. They are silent and motionless for a while.*)

SOLDIER I: John . . .

SOLDIER II: What?

SOLDIER I: Are you alive?

SOLDIER II: Yes. I'm just wounded. . . . And you?

SOLDIER I: Just wounded. . . . (*Pause.*) John . . .

SOLDIER II: What? (*Soldier I points to 105 and 106. Soldier II turns his head cautiously.*) Who are they?

SOLDIER I: (*He points to Soldier II and himself.*) Same thing. . . . Enlisted. . . . (*To 105 and 106.*) How did they get you?

106: We were walking down the street and we heard someone say, "Hey, soldier."

SOLDIER I: And you looked.

SOLDIER II: You shouldn't have looked.

SOLDIER I: Well, they get you anyway. I didn't look, but they hit me on the head, threw me on the barber chair, and here I am . . . waiting for the bombs . . . (*Pause.*) John . . .

SOLDIER II: What?

SOLDIER I: In case I don't make it, drop this in the mail, will you?

SOLDIER II: What is it?

SOLDIER I: A letter.

SOLDIER II: What does it say? (*Soldier I takes the letter out of the envelope and sings.*)

SOLDIER I:

"Sidney N. Phelps, Director.
Dining, sleeping, and parlor car,
Penn Central, Long Island City,
New York, one one one o one.

"Mr. Phelps,
On Tuesday, March seventeenth,
On board The Boston Colonial
Of the Penn Central Railroad
I had the worst hamburger
I ever had;
Served to me on dining car
Four four seven four four.
Mr. Phelps, I've had
Bad hamburgers before,
But that was the worst
I ever had."

SOLDIER II: I'll mail it for you. (*He reaches for the letter but is distracted by the Mayor and Miss Cake's entrance. He carries a picnic basket. She wears a shawl. They walk through serenely and gallantly.*)

MAYOR: My rose, is it too cool for you?

MISS CAKE: No, it's balmy and besides I am wearing my wrap.

MAYOR: It's so nice of you to come with me to review the troops.

MISS CAKE: Don't mention it.

(*The Soldiers, 105 and 106 watch them exit.*)

SOLDIER I:

When Madeline told me it was all off
I took The Boston Colonial,
And as the train pulled off
I looked to see if my Madeline was there
But she wasn't.
Oh, Madeline. Oh, Madeline
Why weren't you there?
Why weren't you there?

(*Bomb. The Mother enters.*)

MOTHER: Have you seen my babies? (*The Soldiers, 105 and 106 shake their heads.*)

They were round and tender. . . . They only spoke two words . . . poles apart. . . . Let me see if I can remember. . . . North-South. . . . No, that's not it. . . . Well, take any two words and say they were it. Have you seen them? (*They shake their heads.*) They had small teeth. Like little grains of rice. And just two . . . in front. . . . You haven't seen them? (*They shake their heads. The Mother exits singing "Two little Angels" sotto-voce. The Mayor and Miss Cake enter.*)

MAYOR: Ah, there you are. I seem to have bypassed you. (*To Miss Cake.*) Here is the platoon, my lily. We bypassed them.

MISS CAKE: Yes, . . . This is where they are . . . and were. (*The Servant enters, running. She carries the loot bag. The Jailer follows her. They circle the Soldiers twice. The Jailer changes direction and grabs the Servant as she runs toward him. She throws the loot bag up in the air. 106 catches it and throws it to 105 as the Jailer goes toward him.*)

MAYOR: Oh, what's happening? Why all the running? (*The bag goes from hand to hand until it falls in the Mayor's hands.*) Oh, a donation for the orphanage . . . from the troops. How timely. I was just thinking I need a new team of horses . . . for my new carriage. (*He gives the Jailer the picnic basket.*) Take this. Go find a nice spot for the picnic, with flowers and a view. And take my damsel to it. Make sure it's a shady spot. The sun makes her blush.

MISS CAKE: Flush.

JAILER: Flush sounds better. I'm sure this lady never blushed. (*The Servant tries to take the bag from the Mayor. He threatens her with the back of his hand. The Ladies and Gentlemen enter in the manner of people at a garden party.*)

MAYOR: What now? Review the troops. Att-ent-ion. There you are . . . standing at attention. Fine bunch. They jump at my command. (*They all jump slightly.*) Ha ha. That's the spirit. Let's see . . . (*Referring to Miss I.*) That's a nice posture, Sergeant. (*Giving her a slap on the back.*) Good boy . . . good boy. Splendid, get his name. (*To Miss O.*) That's a nice uniform, officer, where did you have it made? Shipshape. (*He kisses Miss O on both cheeks.*) You can't tell the men from the women nowadays. But it doesn't matter . . . it does not matter as long as they can shoot. Shoot. Shoot. Nothing wrong with you boys. (*Looking at Miss U.*) Hm, that's a good cannon ball. Yes, shipshape. Everything's in good form. Lucky stiffs. Shoot. Shoot. (*Bomb.*) Oooops. Don't shoot your captain now. Shoot to the side. Ha ha. Yes, sir, pretty field you have here, roses and fireworks. Lucky stiffs, you can have a picnic any time you want. . . . Look at those guns. Great guns. Rifles. That's what you call them. (*Bomb.*) Ooops. What's that noise? I didn't know it was the Fourth of July. . . . Neither did I. Hm. I'm sure I brought someone with me. Where is my damsel?

MISS CAKE: Yooo hoooo. I'm here.

MAYOR: There you are of course (*The Mayor goes to Miss Cake.*)

MISS U: Rompous-mompus-gambol-mumble! (*The music for "Spring is Here" starts.*)

MAYOR: Hmmm. I smell chocolate pudding. . . . Where is it? (*He stands abruptly and runs after the Servant. The Jailer runs after 105 and 106.*)

LADIES: Mompus-mumble-rompous-gambol!

(*The Jailer and the Mayor bump against each other. They start dancing together. Miss Cake dances on the tablecloth. The Ladies and Gentlemen start undoing the Soldiers' head bandages.*)

LADIES & GENTLEMEN: Spring is here!
LADIES:
   Ahaa ahaa ahaa
   Arbutus are here
   And spring beauties.
   Ohoo ohoo ohoo
   It's springtime,
   And hepaticas are blooming.

(*The Ladies and Gentlemen dance around the Soldiers using their head bandages as ribbons around a Maypole.*)

LADIES & GENTLEMEN:
   I see a bride,
   Oohoohoo hoohoohoo
   I see a bride in white.
   Oohoohoo hoohoohoo.
SOLDIER I: Oh, please don't.
LADIES & GENTLEMEN:
   I see a lady,
   I see two,
   I see a groom behind a tree.
   Oohoohoo hoohoohoo.
SOLDIER I: Don't do that. (*Simultaneously with:*)
SOLDIER II: Please don't.
LADIES & GENTLEMEN:
   Come out, come out
   Wherever you are.
   Come out, come out
   Wherever you are.
LADIES: Those who give will get of nature's bounty through the year.
SOLDIER I & SOLDIER II: Oh. (*The Mother starts hitting the dancers.*)
MOTHER: Leave them alone . . .

LADIES & GENTLEMEN:
I see a bride,
Oohoohoo hoohoohoo.
I see a bride in white,
Oohoohoo hoohoohoo.
MOTHER: Leave them alone. Let go.
LADIES & GENTLEMEN:
I see a lady,
I see two.
I see a groom
Behind a tree,
Oohoohoo hoohoohoo.

Apples,
Peaches,
Pumpkin pie.
I see you,
I see you,
Anyone I see is it.
LADIES: Look down a well reflected in a mirror. And you'll see your future
spouse's face.
SOLDIER I: Oh Madeline.

LADIES:	GENTLEMEN:
Ready or not here I come.	Come out, come out
Ready or not here I come.	Come out, come out

SOLDIER I:
I looked to see if my Madeline
Was there.
But she wasn't.
Oh, Madeline, Madeline, Madeline.
Why weren't you there.
LADIES & GENTLEMEN: O, what a fierce and fiery fiesta.

SERVANT, 105, 106:	LADIES, GENTLEMEN:
Riches made them dumb	I see a lady
Riches made them dumb	I see two.

MOTHER: Let them go.
MAYOR: Come to my house everyone. I have plenty of wine, and you people
are a jolly bunch. (*The dancers exit as they sing the following:*)
DANCERS:
Après vous,
Après vous,
Pas du tout.
Je vous en prie.
Mon plaisir.

Le nôtre.
Permettez-moi
Notre plaisir.
Le mien.
A votre service.
Au votre.
Au votre.
L'age avant la beauté.

(The Mother, 105, 106 and the Servant go to the Soldiers. The Mother and the Servant hold them in their arms while 105 and 106 take off their bandages.)

MOTHER: Here. I have something you'll like. (*She looks in her pockets.*) Oh, I forgot to bring it. (*She looks again.*) I always have something in my pockets. Well, I'll tell you a story. . . . There was a man . . . a very wise man who wanted to conquer pain. He tried and tried but he couldn't find a way. . . . One day he went fishing just to distract himself from this thought that occupied his mind. . . . He caught one fish and then another . . . and as he sat there waiting for the next fish to bite, he suddenly said, "I got it! You conquer pain the way you catch a fish. When pain bites you don't look away. You pull it toward you. And when it's right on top of you, and it starts flapping, and almost knocking you down, that's when you have it conquered, because it's out of the water." Yes, that's what he said.

105 & 106:
When I was born I opened my eyes,
And when I looked around I closed them;
And when I saw how people get kicked in the head,
And kicked in the belly, and kicked in the groin,
I closed them.
My eyes are closed but I'm carefree.
Ho ho ho, ho ho ho, I'm carefree.

105:
A poor man has fifty problems every day
Fifty problems upon opening his eyes,
Fifty problems every minute of the day.
And life is sour.
One thing a poor man has,
That a rich man doesn't have,
Is fifty problems every day.

When a wound is open
And the guts are hanging out,
It hurts.
And it hurts as much

When a man's life
Is dark and narrow.

A poor man doesn't know
Where his pain comes from.
There is a dark wall,
And a closed door,
And a dirty old room,
And he doesn't know how he got there.

A poor man's life is sour
And he doesn't know
Who made it so.

106:

A poor man has to do what he's told.
He doesn't know just why he does it.
He just has to do what he's told.

Do the dirty work.
Get off the street.
It's you who has to fight the war.

He gets kicked in the head,
And kicked in the belly,
And kicked in the groin,

I know what madness is.
It's not knowing how another man feels.
A madman has never been
In another man's shoes.

Madness is lack of compassion,
And there's little compassion
In the world.

It's only stupid things
That make a madman feel sure:
Money, power, adulation;
Never just being alive,
Having two feet on the ground,
And having heart to give.

105 & 106:

When I was born I opened my eyes,
And when I looked around I closed them;
And when I saw how people get kicked in the head,
And kicked in the belly, and kicked in the groin,
I closed them.
My eyes are closed but I'm carefree.

Ho ho ho, ho ho ho, I'm carefree.

(*The Soldiers feel their healed bodies.*)

SOLDIER II: I feel better.
SOLDIER I: I do too.
SOLDIER II: Let's go to the Mayor's party.
MOTHER: I don't want to go to the Mayor's party.
SOLDIER II: Why not?
MOTHER: I don't like him. (*Soldier II beckons the Servant. She shakes her head.*)
SOLDIER II: (*To 105 and 106.*) There'll be wine there. (*They shake their heads. He goes to Soldier I and punches him lightly. Soldier I shakes his head. The music to "Why Not" starts. Soldier II starts dancing. He turns to the Mother.*) Come . . . (*He leads the Mother in a simple dance.*)
SOLDIER I, II, THE SERVANT & THE MOTHER:
  La la la
  La la la
  La la la
  La la la
(*He beckons the Servant once more.*)
SERVANT:
  Why not? Why not?
  Let's go and have some fun
  Why not?
  If we can dance and have some fun;
  If there's free wine.
  We're a jolly bunch.

(*The Mother and Soldier II start exiting doing the same dance step. Soldier I and the Servant join them.*)

SOLDIER I, II, THE SERVANT & THE MOTHER:
  Why not?
  Why not?
  Why not?
  Why not!

(*105 and 106 follow them. They are downcast.*)

SCENE 2

(*The Mayor's Drawing Room. The Mayor sits on a high chair. A stethoscope hangs from his neck. The Jailer and Miss Cake stand by his sides. The rest enter in the order they left the previous scene.*)

MAYOR: Welcome. . . . Welcome. . . . I am about to entertain. Whoever is not amused will be sent to the common cell.

JAILER: Hear, hear. The show is about to start.

MAYOR: Have any of you ever heard the story of the rabbit and the turtle?

ALL: Yes.

MAYOR: You see, it goes like this: There was once a rabbit who said to the turtle: "Run fast. Run fast, or I'll win the race." "I'll run slowly," said the turtle, "and win the race." "If that is the case, I'll take a rest," said the rabbit. "Who are you to give me advantages?" said the turtle. And so on . . . and so on . . . and so on. Whoever doesn't laugh will be sent to the common cell. (*They all laugh reluctantly.*) Good. Now the party's over. Let me see what time it is. (*Looking at his watch.*) Too late! Everybody's under arrest for keeping me up so late. Wait, you've been reprieved. My watch stopped. It must be earlier than I thought. Or later. Amuse yourselves. I give the best parties in town. I don't? Who said that? I must be hearing things again. No one would dare say I don't give the best parties in town. Now, who has some mighty good entertainment? (*Mr. R, Mr. S and Mr. T walk to the center in a vaudevillian manner.*)

MR. R: This is my son. (*Apologetically.*) He needs a haircut.

MR. S: What he needs is a new face. (*Mr. R, Mr. S, and Mr. T laugh heartily.*)

MAYOR: Pretty dull. Pretty dull. I have seen better entertainment than that. You better do something funny, or I'll tell you another story. (*Mr. R steps forward.*)

MR. R:
Whenever my fingers went like this,
I said: "Hell, my fingers always go like that."
Until one day somebody said to me:
"How original it is that your fingers go like that."

Since then, every time my fingers go like this,
I say: "Look at my fingers go like that.
How original it is that my fingers go like this."
One of these days I'll sell them. (*They applaud.*)

MAYOR: That's nothing! I wouldn't buy your fingers if you paid me. Why, I remember the days when I could do all kinds of things with my fingers and my mother used to say to me, "Why Jennifer, you're being salacious." Ha ha. (*They all laugh reluctantly.*) Who's next? (*Mr. T takes out a song sheet. He gets the key from the piano and sings:*)

MR. T:
It is true I told you I would love you
And I never did.
But remember, I'm forgetful,
Little fool.
Longings are like vapor.
They go as they come.

And remember, little fool,
I'm forgetful.

Both my wife's and my mistress' name is Kate.
One day, while I made love to Kate, my wife,
I thought of my sweet mistress Kate.
In a moment of passion and confusion,
I said: "Kate, dear Kate, oh, Kate."
My wife, hearing me speak my mistress' name,
Said harsh words to me, and put me on the street.
Is that fair, I ask you, is that fair?

It is true, I told you I would love you,
And I never did.
But remember, I'm forgetful,
Little fool.

ALL:
Longings are like vapor.
They go as they come.

MR. T:
And remember, little fool,
I'm forgetful.

(*They all applaud. The servant does a dance to the accompaniment of the "Czardas.". Others play instruments, do head stands, kazatskis, and different tricks according to the actor's ability.*)

MAYOR: No good. No good. That's common and ordinary. I'm a poet and a scholar. Let's hear some poetry.

105: Miss Cake?

MISS CAKE: Yes, Mr. 105.

105: What do you aim at in your work?

MISS CAKE: Magic.

106: Do you always achieve it?

MISS CAKE: Yes. Once in a while.

106: You don't mean always, then.

MISS CAKE: Yes, I do.

105: Explain.

MISS CAKE: In mathematical terms, if the impossible is ever achieved, it becomes always. That is how eternity is conceived.

MAYOR: That makes sense. But it's not poetry. Go back to your cake. Now, this is poetry.

A petunia is a flower like a begonia.
You fry begonia like you fry sausage.

Sausage and battery is a crime.
Monkeys crime trees.
Tree is a crowd.
The cock crowd and made a noise.
You have a noise on your face, also two eyes.
The opposite of ayes is nays.
A horse nays and has a colt.
You go to bed with a colt,
And wake up with double petunia.

Whoever doesn't laugh will be sent to the common cell.

(*All except 105 and 106 sing the "Laughing Song." The Mayor uses his stethoscope to make sure they are all laughing. At the end of the song he reaches 105 and 106. To the Jailer:*)

Take them away. (*As the Jailer takes 105 and 106 away, the Mother takes a few steps toward them.*)
MOTHER: Don't take my children away.

Does anyone understand a mother's love?
Except a mother?
Does a father understand a mother's love?
Except a good father?
Does anyone understand a mother's love?
Except a son, or a grandfather, or an uncle?
ALL: Everyone.
MOTHER: (*Recitative.*)
Then do you know that one autumn afternoon
My children disappeared and that that very
Autumn afternoon my life ended?
(*The Jailer re-enters with 105 and 106.*)
JAILER: I went the wrong way. That's the kitchen. (*He walks in the opposite direction.*)
MOTHER: Oh . . . I must kill myself. (*The Mother pantomimes reaching for a knife and stabbing herself. She falls to the ground.*)
MAYOR: Marvelous . . . marvelous. That's good entertainment. Do it again. (*The Mother stands and repeats the same motions.*) Marvelous. Now the party is over. Let me see what time it is. Too late! Everybody's under arrest for keeping me up so late. Good night. That was mighty good entertainment. (*The Jailer takes everyone to jail. The Mayor waves.*) I must remember that. (*He tries to remember the Mother's movements. The lights fade.*)

SCENE 3

(*The Cell. It is empty. There is the sound of voices. All except the Mayor enter.*)

THE JAILER: The ladies are to come with me to the next cell . . . one at a time. It's too crowded here.

MISS O: Yes, it's too crowded here. I am not having fun.

MR. T: Don't push, Miss I. There is no place to go. (*To Mr. S.*) You are stepping on my toe.

MR. S: Who said that being arrested could be fun?

MISS I: Well, it's not all that it's made up to be. It's a bore.

MISS U: I like it.

MR. R: She likes it. Why do you like it?

MISS U: It's different.

MR. R: You're sticking your elbow in my back, Miss O.

MISS O: I can't help it. I'm being pushed.

MR. R: Well, don't bend your arm. Keep it straight. (*Miss O straightens her arm.*)

MR. S: Oops. Who did that?

MR. T: I'm going home. Make way.

MISS O: Me too.

JAILER: You can't go home. You're under arrest. (*Mr. T and Miss O exit through the hole.*)

MR. S: Little man, step aside. (*The Jailer steps aside. All except the Mother, the Servant, 105 and 106 begin to exit.*)

MR. R: Let's call Mr. Lipschitz.

MR. S: Let's play croquet. At night you don't know if the ball went under the wicket.

MISS O: Oh, let's play it on my lawn. I don't even have a set.

MISS I: Fickle. . . . (*The Jailer exits through the door and locks it.*)

JAILER: Well, whoever is left is under arrest. (*He exits.*)

SERVANT: Sure. (*Pause.*) Well . . . I'll go now. . . .

MOTHER: Where will you go?

SERVANT: I don't know . . . I'll go for a walk.

MOTHER: Will you be all right?

SERVANT: Yes, it's almost morning. The city is quiet now.

MOTHER: Be careful.

SERVANT: I'll be careful. (*To 105 and 106.*) Good night, friends.

105 & 106: Good night.

SERVANT: I'll be seeing you.

105 & 106: Would you like us to go with you?

SERVANT: No. I . . . It's okay. I'd like to be alone . . . and think.

105 & 106: We'll see you soon. . . .

SERVANT: Very soon. (*The door opens for her. She steps out of the cell and turns to wave. They wave back. She exits.*)

MOTHER: Well, it's time to go to sleep now.

105 & 106: Yes.

MOTHER: Did you have a good time, my children?

105 & 106: Yes.

MOTHER: Did you find evil?

105 & 106: No.

MOTHER: Good night, then. Sleep well. You'll find it some other time.

105 & 106: Good night. (*The Mother rocks them to sleep.*)

MOTHER:

I saw a man lying in the street,
Asleep and drunk.
He had not washed his face.
He held his coat closed with a safety pin
And I thought, and I thought
Thank God, I'm better than he.

I have to live with my own truth,
I have to live with it.
You live with your own truth,
I cannot live with it.
I have to live with my own truth,
Whether you like it or not,
Whether you like it or not.

There are many poor people in the world,
Whether you like it or not.
There are many poor people in the world.
But I'm not one of them.
I'm not one of them.
Someone's been stealing my apples
But I'm not one of them,
I'm not one of them.

I know everything.
Half of it I really know,
The rest I make up,
The rest I make up.
Some things I'm sure of,
Of other things I'm too sure,
And of others I'm not sure at all.
People believe everything they hear,
Not what they see, not what they see.
People believe everything they hear;
But me, I see everything.
Yes, I see everything.

The saddest day of my life was the day
That I pitied a despicable man.
And I've been sad ever since,
Yes, I've been sad ever since.

I'd like to go where a human being
Is not a strange thing,
Is not a strange thing.

When I go, no one will water my plants.
When I go, no one will water my plants.
No one . . . no one . . . no one . . .

Yes, my children, you'll find evil . . . some other time. Good night. (*She exits.*)

105 & 106: Good night.

All is well in the city.
People do what they want.
They can go to the park.
They can sleep all they want.
And for those who have no cake,
There's plenty of bread.

END

The Successful Life of 3

To Susan Sontag

The Successful Life of 3 was first presented at the Firehouse Theatre in Minneapolis on January 22, 1965. It was directed and designed by the author, with the following cast:

He:	*Jeff Moses*
She:	*Carrie Bartlett*
3:	*Mel Semler*
Policemen and Bodyguards:	*Don Young, Edd Ward, Mike Monson*

The play was subsequently presented by the Open Theatre at the Sheridan Square Playhouse in New York on March 15, 1965. This production was directed initially by Joseph Chaikin, and then re-directed by Richard Gilman, with the following cast:

He:	*James Barbosa*
She:	*Barbara Vann*
3:	*Paul Boesing*
Policemen and Bodyguards:	*Sydney Schubert Walter, Ron Faber, Rhea Gaisner*

CHARACTERS:

He, a handsome young man
She, a sexy young lady
3, a plump, middle-aged man
Bodyguards
Policemen

*** following a character's name indicates:

For She, that she thinks with a stupid expression (the others watch her).
For He, that he looks disdainful (the others watch him).
And for 3, that 3 looks with intense curiosity (the others watch him).
Deadpan.

SCENE 1

(*The Doctor's Office. 3 and He sit. He is combing his hair. 3 takes a shoe off and drops it. At the sound of the shoe, He becomes motionless, his arms suspended in the air. 3 looks at He and freezes for a moment.*)

3: What are you doing?

HE: Waiting.

3: What for?

HE: For the other shoe to drop.

3: Ah, and I was wondering what you were doing. If I hadn't asked, we would have stayed like that forever. You waiting and me wondering . . . That's the kind of person I am. I ask . . . That's good, you know.

HE: Why?

3: ***

HE: Why?

3: It starts action.

HE: What action did you start?

3: We're talking.

HE: That's nothing. We could as well be waiting for the shoe to drop. (*He suspends his arms in the air again. 3 stares at He. They remain motionless for a while.*)

3: Sorry . . . I'm going to do my sewing.

HE: First take the other shoe off. Get it over with.

3: (*Taking off his shoe.*) I wasn't going to take it off. (*3 takes needle and thread and sews a button on his shirt.*) You see? If I do it now I don't have to do it later.

HE: What?

3: The sewing.

HE: And what are you going to do later?

3: *** (*Puts the needle and thread away.*) Look, there are advantages to being optimistic.

HE: Sure.

3: What are they?

HE: You tell me.

3: Well, it makes one feel happier.

HE: You don't look happy to me.

3: Oh, no?

HE: No.

3: Well, things are not what they appear to the eye.

HE: They aren't?

3: Are they?

HE: Sometimes . . . sometimes they are just what they appear to the eye . . . Don't generalize.

3: Why?

HE: Because there are always exceptions. There's always one that isn't like the others.

3: If it's just one, it can be thrown in with the rest. It doesn't matter.

HE: It matters.

3: Perhaps you can exclude it in your mind. Without mentioning it.

HE: You have to mention it . . . You're splitting hairs anyway.

3: I like splitting hairs.

HE: Well, do it when I'm not around.

3: I was just joking.

HE: (*Correcting him.*) Being facetious.

3: (*Taking an apple from his pocket.*) Want an apple?

HE: No.

3: An apple a day keeps the doctor away.

HE: I knew you were going to say that. (*She enters wearing a nurse's uniform.*) Miss, you're a fine dish.

SHE: Thanks. (*She exits and re-enters.*)

HE: Miss, I would like to bounce on you.

SHE: Thank you. (*To 3.*) Come in please. (*3 and She exit. She re-enters.*)

HE: Miss, I would like to bang you.

SHE: Your friend just did.

HE: Well, I'm next.

SHE: I only do it once a day.

HE: I get you all worked up and you do it with him instead?

SHE: ***

HE: I'm handsome and sexy and I get you all worked up, and you go and do it with him? Answer now.

SHE: What?

HE: Is that natural?

SHE: I don't know. (*3 enters.*)

HE: A moment ago I was thinking of marrying you.

SHE: You just saw me for the first time.

3: He figured he'd see you a few more times if he married you.

HE: Don't speak for me after you ruined everything . . . Let me try again. Miss, would you go to the movies with me after work?

SHE: Okay, I like the movies.

HE: Everybody likes the movies.

SHE: I never liked them until a few months ago.

HE: What made you like them then?

SHE: I saw a movie with the Lane sisters.

HE: You like them?

SHE: Yes, they're all right.

HE: What do they do?

SHE: Stupid things.

HE: Like what?

SHE: They cry and laugh.

HE: That doesn't sound so great.

SHE: I like it. It's all right if you like sisters.

3: I like movies about marriage, divorce and remarriage.

SHE: I like sisters.

HE: I don't have any particular preference. I just like good movies . . . with action and a lot of killing.

SHE: I couldn't go to the movies if I didn't have a preference.

3: Neither could I. (*3 takes She by the hand and exits. She re-enters.*)

HE: Did you make it with him again?

SHE: Yes.

HE: How long are you going to keep this up?

SHE: I don't know. (*3 re-enters.*)

HE: Listen, I was even thinking of marrying you.

SHE: You'd have to give me a ring for that. Two rings. An engagement ring and a wedding band.

3: I'll give the bride away.

HE: From the looks of it you're not leaving anything to give away.

3: And I'm not through yet.

HE: I didn't say you were.

3: You didn't say I was but you sure wish I were.

SHE: Me too.

HE: I never wish.

SHE: In my profession you have to wish.

3: For what?

SHE: ***

HE: I don't have a profession.

SHE: How are you going to support me?

HE: I'll find a way.

3: He sure does have to support you. Doesn't he?

SHE: Yeah, my parents pay for the wedding and he supports me.

3: I'll pay for the wedding.

HE: He doesn't have any money. Get your parents to pay for the wedding.

SHE: Weddings are a pain in the neck.

3: Why do you want one then?

SHE: ***

HE: Don't you see she doesn't know?

3: Yes, I see.

SHE: The Andrews sisters are all married.

HE: Do you like brothers too?

SHE: Not so much.

HE: Did you see *The Corsican Brothers?*

SHE: That's not brothers. That's just Douglas Fairbanks playing twins. It's not the same.

HE: What brothers do you like?

SHE: I don't know any.

HE: How do you know you like them?

SHE: ***

3: She didn't say she liked them.

HE: Didn't you say you like them?

SHE: No, I said, "Not so much" . . . I don't think I'm going to marry you.

3: Why?

HE: I can ask my own questions, if you please. (*To She.*) Why?

SHE: You're too picky.

HE: That's all right. Are we going to the movies or not?

SHE: Sure.

3: If you find a sister movie.

SHE: That's all right. I'll try another kind.

3: Let's go in for a quickie before you leave. (*3 and She exit. She re-enters wearing a hat.*)

HE: Ready?

SHE: Yes.

HE: Hey, didn't you say you only do it once a day?

SHE: Yes.

HE: How come you did it with him three times already?

SHE: ***

HE: You're not a liar, are you?
SHE: No.
HE: You better not be, because I can't stand liars. (*3 re-enters. He and She exit.*)
3: Wait for me. (*3 exits.*)

SCENE 2

(*The movies. The lights go down and flicker. He, 3 and She enter. They sit—3 in the middle, She and He at his sides.*)

HE: Hey, what do you mean by sitting next to her? Change with me. She's my date.
3: I can't feel her up from there.
HE: You don't have to feel her up. (*3 and He change seats.*)
3: How about some popcorn?
SHE: I'll go.
3: Don't go. Let him go.
HE: You go.
3: I can't. (*He exits. 3 moves next to She. He re-enters.*)
HE: Move back to your seat.
3: I already moved once. I'm not moving twice. Let's have some popcorn. (*He offers popcorn to 3.*) I'll hold it because I'm in the middle. (*3 tries to hold the bag, eat popcorn, and feel She up.*) You hold the bag. I can't feel her up and eat at the same time if I hold the bag. (*He takes the bag.*)
HE: At least wait till the feature starts.

SCENE 3

(*The porch. Ten years later. He dozes. She peels potatoes. 3 sews.*)

SHE: I'm going to divorce him.
3: Give him another chance.
SHE: Him?
3: He's not bad.
SHE: Yes, he is.
3: There are worse.
SHE: No, there aren't.
3: Wouldn't it be worse if you were married to me?
SHE: What difference would it make?
3: It would make a difference.
SHE: No, it wouldn't.
3: Yes, it would.
SHE: What difference?

3: ***

SHE: What difference?

3: I'll ask him. (*3 shakes He.*) Hey, would it make any difference if she was married to me instead of you?

HE: Yeah.

3: What difference?

HE: Ask her. She ought to know.

3: She doesn't know.

HE: She never knows anything.

3: Actually, this time she knows. She said it wouldn't make any difference.

HE: She's probably right, because she usually doesn't know anything.

SHE: I'm going to divorce him whether I'm right or wrong.

3: Marry a worse one for a while . . . then remarry him and you'll be happier.

HE: That would be like wearing tight shoes so it feels better when you take them off.

3: That's the idea. Do it.

SHE: You can't do that.

3: Why not?

SHE: I don't know.

3: (*To He.*) Do you know why you can't wear tight shoes so it feels better when you take them off?

HE: No.

SHE: But isn't it true that you're not supposed to?

HE: Yeah.

SHE: I knew it.

3: Well, you'd be happier if you did it.

SHE: You're not supposed to.

HE: (*To 3.*) Get off that chair. I want to put my feet up. (*3 moves to another chair.*)

3: Rivalry.

SHE: What?

3: Rivalry.

SHE: ***

3: Masculine rivalry.

SHE: ***

3: Masculine rivalry. (*3 points to He and to himself.*)

SHE: Who ever heard of such a thing.

3: What?

SHE: What you said.

3: Rivalry?

SHE: Yeah.

3: You haven't heard of it?

SHE: No.

3: I bet you he has. (*To He.*) Have you heard of rivalry?

HE: Sure.

3: See?

SHE: I mean the other.

3: Masculine?

SHE: Both, both together.

3: (*To He.*) Have you heard of masculine rivalry?

HE: Yeah.

SHE: So he has. (*3 looks She over.*)

3: I don't desire you any more.

SHE: Thank God.

3: Don't thank God. Thank me.

SHE: Stop picking on me.

HE: Are you picking on her again?

3: I can't help it.

HE: Stop picking on her.

3: Masculine rivalry.

HE: What are you talking about? There's no comparison. I'm sexy and you're slimy.

SHE: That's the only thing I like about him.

HE: You like *that*

SHE: It's all right . . . But I'm tired of having children.

HE: That's not true. You told me you like children.

SHE: Not that many.

3: How many are there?

SHE: I don't know.

3: How do you know there are too many?

SHE: ***

3: I'll go count them. (*3 exits.*)

HE: Listen, you can't one day say you like babies and the next day say you don't.

SHE: Why not?

HE: You have to make up your mind.

SHE: *** (*She doesn't answer.*)

HE: Well?

SHE: I can't stand the twins.

HE: Why not?

SHE: They look too much alike.

HE: Twins always do.

SHE: I didn't say they didn't.

HE: You didn't say they did either.

SHE: No, all I said was that I didn't like them.

HE: Why?

SHE: I don't see why they have to dress alike.

HE: Twins always do.
SHE: I didn't say they didn't.
HE: Bring the food out.
SHE: There's no food.
HE: How come?
SHE: You know how come.
HE: No, I don't.
SHE: You're supposed to provide for me, but you don't.
HE: Don't I get you all the potatoes?
SHE: I'm going. I can't stand peeling potatoes all the time. (*She exits. 3 enters.*)
HE: She left.
3: Oh.
HE: That's all right. I never want what I don't have.
3: I missed it.
HE: What?
3: Her leaving. I've been waiting around to see her leave, and now she does it when I'm not looking. How did she go?
HE: ***

SCENE 4

(*The porch. Three years later. He peels potatoes, 3 sews.*)

3: I'm going into business. I can't stand this home life any longer.
HE: You wouldn't be any good at it.
3: I might as well try it.
HE: You would just lose all your money.
3: I don't have any money.
HE: How're you going to go into business?
3: I'll put a bid on some nylon rope, go south, convince the fishermen to use nylon instead of whatever they use, take the orders, come north, get the rope, go south, and take them for all they've got.
HE: They probably use nylon.
3: Then I'll sell it to them cheap and still make a fortune.
HE: It wouldn't work.
3: No? . . . Well, I can make a sandwich with peanut butter and Ritz crackers, dip it in chocolate, call it Tootsie Tootsie, and sell it.
HE: You're better off with the nylon rope.
3: I thought so too. I'll go try it.
HE: Okay.
3: Goodbye. Give my love to Ruth if you see her. Have you seen her?
HE: Yes, she's happily married.
3: Who to?

HE: I don't know.

3: Well, if you see her, tell her I would still like a roll in the hay with her, even if she's getting old and decrepit.

HE: Okay, I'll tell her.

3: Goodbye. You do think it will work.

HE: Sure.

3: Goodbye then. (*3 exits.*)

HE: Just said that to get rid of him.

3: (*Re-enters, wearing top hat and furs.*) It worked.

HE: Don't tell me it worked.

3: (*Respectfully.*) Oh, sorry.

HE: What do you mean it worked?

3: I put a bid on some nylon rope, went south, convinced them fishermen to use nylon instead of whatever they were using, and took them for all they had. D'you know rope is sold by the weight, not by the measure?

HE: Don't get smart with me, Arthur. I'm very annoyed. I have all the brains and the looks and it's you who goes south with your squeaky voice and sweaty hands and makes all the money.

3: And I'm not finished yet. I'm going to make that peanut butter sandwich and make another mint.

HE: You're making me sick.

3: Don't get sick yet. I'm just starting. You think Ruth likes money?

HE: Sure.

3: Perhaps she'll come live with us for the money. It'll be good for the children.

HE: I'm the husband and the father. I'll make my own decisions.

3: Yeah, but I do all the screwing and make all the money.

HE: Don't rub it in.

3: Sorry.

HE: You may make all the money and all that, but you have no manners.

3: Teach me manners. (*He puts on the top hat and furs. She enters.*)

SHE: Okay, I came back.

HE: Because of the money.

SHE: I like money.

HE: Everybody likes money. You say it as if it was something special.

SHE: It is special. I like money very much.

3: More than sisters?

SHE: ***

HE: Never mind.

3: I have a present for you. (*3 gives She three men's hats.*)

SHE: These are men's hats. What's the matter with you?

3: Nothing.

HE: He doesn't know his ass from his elbow.

3: I do. (*3 points to his buttocks and his elbow.*) I only didn't know what kind of hat to buy.

SHE: Where's the money?

3: In the bank.

SHE: Oh, damn it. I came for the money and you put it away.

HE: You didn't come for that. You didn't come for that. You came for me and the children.

SHE: You said I came for the money.

HE: I was just accusing you.

SHE: And what was I supposed to say?

HE: "I didn't. I didn't. I came for you and the children." Defend yourself.

SHE: Well, I didn't.

HE: I don't have to stay here while you come back for his money. I'm sexy and bright and you're a bunch of morons. I'm leaving. (*3 puts his arm around She.*) You don't have to jump on her the moment I turn my back. (*3 lets go of She.*)

SHE: I'm glad he caught you.

HE: You can do what you want. I'm leaving. Goodbye. (*He exits.*)

SHE: What are we going to do without him?

3: Wait for him.

SCENE 5

(*The store. Three years later. He is standing. 3 steals a pipe.*)

HE: Arthur!

3: What are you doing here?

HE: I'm a store detective.

3: How long have you been a store detective?

HE: Since I left the house.

3: Is the pay good?

HE: Not for the risk you take.

3: What risk?

HE: You might get hit or knifed.

3: Who would do that?

HE: The thief. You see, I grab him like this. I identify myself and I tell him to go with me to the office. Then he either becomes frightened and comes along quietly, or becomes violent and attacks me. (*3 punches He and runs.*)

SCENE 6

(*The porch. A few minutes later. She peels potatoes. 3 enters smoking the pipe.*)

3: I just saw him. He's a detective.

SHE: I don't like detectives.

3: Why?

SHE: I can't understand them.

3: Why not?

SHE: They talk too fast.

3: He's a store detective. They don't talk fast.

SHE: A store detective is not a real detective.

3: Someone stole something though.

SHE: Did he figure out who did it?

3: I don't know. I hit him and ran.

SHE: You didn't run so fast. You're late for dinner. . . . Did you figure out who
   did it?

3: Yeah, I did it.

SHE: What did you do?

3: (*Showing her the pipe.*) Stole it. (*He enters.*)

HE: Why did you hit me?

SHE: Is that a way to come in after you've been gone for three years? Can't
   you say hello?

HE: I don't feel like saying hello.

SHE: You could at least pretend.

HE: Why did you hit me?

3: Because I had to.

HE: Why?

3: Because I'm the thief and you're the detective.

HE: What did you steal?

3: Guess.

HE: I give up.

3: The pipe.

HE: Now I have to take you in.

3: You have to identify yourself.

HE: Don't be silly. You know me. Come on.

3: Goodbye, Ruth.

SHE: Goodbye.

SCENE 7

(*The porch. Three days later. She and He are sitting.*)

SHE: How come you came back now?

HE: Because he's away. . . . Masculine rivalry.

SHE: That's what he always says.

HE: So what. It's true.

SHE: How come he was stealing?

HE: He didn't know he could take the money out of the bank.

SHE: Can he?

HE: Yeah.

3: (*Enters wearing a prisoner's uniform.*) I organized a revolt and got out.

HE: Can't you stay put in one place?

3: Can't I?

HE: No, you're always jumping from place to place.

3: I'll stay put now. Ruth, even if you're getting old and decrepit, I still want you. Jail makes a man want a woman.

HE: You disgust me. You spend three days in jail and you don't learn anything.

3: I did so. I organized the prisoners and now I'm the head of the mob. If you want I'll make you my bodyguard.

HE: You call that a body?

3: I know. I have to do some exercise. But in the meantime I'll call it a body.

HE: It is not all right with me. I'm leaving.

SHE: He's always leaving.

3: Like Shane . . . Stay and have some fun. The guys are coming presently.

HE: What kind of idiot are you that says presently?

3: No idiot. I'm the Alec Guinness-type gangster.

HE: God damn it. I'm getting fed up. You have no style, no looks, you act like an old housewife, and it's you who gets to go to jail and become the head of the mob.

SHE: Let's eat.

HE: Okay, but if you want me to be your bodyguard, you have to give me a good salary . . . No. I don't care if you get slugged. Goodbye. (*He exits.*)

3: You be my bodyguard, Ruth.

SHE: Okay, but I don't move from this chair.

3: You have to move. You have to keep an eye on me.

SHE: Skip it. Who wants to look at you all the time.

3: Okay. Don't be my bodyguard. I'll get the guys to look after me.

SCENE 8

(*The porch. Six months later. 3 and She sit. 3 is armed to the teeth. Bodyguards surround him.*)

3: I have a sweet streak in me.

SHE: Where?

3: ***

SHE: What did you say?

3: I have a sweet streak in me.

SHE: Me too.

3: I'm tired of the life of crime.

SHE: Why don't you stop stealing?

3: I like stealing.

SHE: I thought you said you were tired of crime.

3: Yes, but not of stealing.

SHE: You're not supposed to steal.

3: Says who?

SHE: ***

3: You don't know anything. I'm going to steal from the rich and give to the poor.

SHE: I came back for the money and you're going to give it to the poor? I'm leaving.

3: Where are you going?

SHE: I'll go find a Joan Fontaine movie.

3: What good would that do you?

SHE: She's Olivia de Havilland's sister.

3: No, she's not.

SHE: Yes, she is.

3: They don't look alike.

SHE: The Lane sisters don't look alike either.

3: No, but they act like sisters.

SHE: ***

(3 exits. She stands puzzled.)

SCENE 9

(The store. A few minutes later. He is standing. 3 walks by surrounded by bodyguards.)

HE: Come with me to the office. You penny-pinching sonofabitch hoodlum. I finally caught you.

3: What for? I just came to get a Zorro costume. *(3 puts on a Zorro costume.)*

HE: You look like an idiot, like you always did. Did you steal it?

3: I bought it.

HE: Show me the sales slip.

3: I lost it.

HE: You stole it. *(To the bodyguards.)* Did he steal it?

BODYGUARDS: Yeah.

HE: Come with me.

3: Don't be silly. If I'm Zorro and the store is rich, I have to steal from it. Now I have to give something to the poor. Here's a penny.

HE: I'm turning you in anyway. I'll get fired if I don't catch someone soon . . . I haven't caught anyone since the last time I caught you. Get moving.

3: No, I won't. I have better things to do, like ride around the pampas with my mask on. Come with me and you can ride too.

HE: What kind of idiot d'you think I am. You'll make me do all the riding and cut all the Z's and you'll get all the credit. You do your own dirty work.

3: No, I won't . . . I'm getting too old to ride around like an idiot.

HE: You used to do your own dirty work.

3: Yeah. But now I'm rich and lazy. (*To a bodyguard.*) Can you ride? (*Bodyguard shakes his head.*) Can you ride? (*Bodyguard shakes his head.*) Get out of my way. I don't need you any more. (*To He.*) Can Ruth ride?

HE: No, she can't do anything.

3: That's all right. I'll go to some rodeo and get myself a double. (*3 exits.*)

SCENE 10

(*The porch. Three days later. He sits. 3 enters panting.*)

3: Hide me.

HE: What from?

3: I'm being followed.

HE: What did you do?

3: I got tired of stealing from the rich and giving to the poor and started stealing from the rich and the poor. Hide me.

HE: I won't hide you. I don't care if they catch you.

3: Hide my *antifaz* then.

HE: What's that?

3: My mask. Do you know that Zorro means fox in Spanish?

HE: Never mind. I don't care if Zorro means fox. I can't hide your *antifaz*. I'll lose my job if I get caught with stolen goods.

3: I thought they were going to fire you.

HE: I caught a girl who didn't do anything and they let me stay.

3: That's not nice. Where's Ruth?

HE: She went to see Joan Fontaine and never came back.

3: Did she take any money with her?

HE: She doesn't need money. She married the guy who owns the movie.

3: How're the children?

HE: They're all right. They're always playing doctor.

3: Are they sick?

HE: No, they just play doctor. (*The Policemen enter and grab 3.*)

3: Where're you taking me?

POLICEMEN: To the scaffold.

3: Oh! Merciful God. (*The Policemen take 3 away. 3 re-enters, carrying a bouquet.*)

HE: I thought they were going to hang you.

3: I got out of it. Here's Ruth. She must have broken up with that movie man. (*She enters. 3 gives her the flowers.*)

SHE: How did you know I was coming?

3: I didn't.

HE: How did you get out?

3: I told them you did it.

HE: I'll lose my job at the store.

3: Don't let that worry you. You won't need a job any more. They're coming back to get you any minute. (*To She.*) What made you come back?

SHE: I'm old and tired and I've had too many men. I'm just going to sit here and rest for the rest of my life.

3: Oh no you won't. You have to work for your keep. Scrub the floor.

HE: I'm going to the store. I can't stand seeing my wife scrubbing floors.

SHE: Don't go. I'm not going to scrub no floors. You've become a mean old sonofabitch, Arthur.

3: I was always mean. I just didn't know it.

SHE: You're not supposed to be mean.

3: Why not?

SHE: ***

HE: She's right. You're not supposed to be mean.

SHE: I knew it.

3: Well, perhaps I just have a mean streak in me.

SHE: Yeah, like the Grand Canyon.

HE: The Grand Canyon is not a streak.

SHE: What is it?

3: It's a ditch.

SHE: Same thing.

3: Well, here are the cops anyway. They're coming to get you.

HE: You're disgusting. You go around being a son of a bitch and then you pin it on me. What am I going to do now?

3: ***

SHE: ***

HE: You're a bunch of morons. (*The Policemen enter. They grab 3.*)

3: Where are you taking me?

POLICEMEN: To the scaffold.

3: I just came from there. (*The Policemen take 3 away.*)

SHE: Are you going to miss him?

HE: No, he's a son of a bitch—are you?

SHE: What?

HE: Going to miss him?

SHE: ***

(*3 enters with a bouquet of flowers and gives them to She.*)

HE: How come you always come back with flowers?

3: They have them there.

SHE: What for?

3: For the grave.

HE: Did you steal them?

3: No, they give them to you.

SHE: They go bad if they don't use them.

HE: How did you get away this time?

3: They caught the real Zorro.

SHE: I thought you were the real Zorro.

3: No, I'm too young.

HE: Bring in the food, Ruth.

SHE: What food?

3: I have some Tootsie Tootsies. (*They eat Tootsie Tootsies. A Policeman enters. 3 shoots him dead.*) I'm not armed to the teeth for nothing. (*They freeze for a moment. Then they sing the "Song to Ignorance."*)

ALL:
> Let me be wrong
> But also not know it.
> Be wrong,
> Be wrong,
> And, oh, not to know it.
> Oh! Let me be wrong.

3:
> One day while walking
> Down the street,
> I found a petunia
> And took it.
> I took it.
> Oh! Let me be wrong.

ALL:
> Let me be wrong.
> But also not know it.
> Be wrong,
> Be wrong,
> And, oh, not to know it.
> Oh! Let me be wrong.

SHE:
> I went from here

HE:
> To where?

SHE:
> I don't know where.
> I called a parasol an umbrella.

Yes, an umbrella.
Oh, let me be wrong.
I don't care.

ALL:

Let me be wrong.
But also not know it.
Be wrong,
Be wrong,
And, oh, not to know it.
Oh! Let me be wrong.

HE:

I sprechen sie dutch very well
I said to Herr Auber:
Herr Auber, I sprechen sie
Dutch very well, Herr Auber.
Oh! Let me be wrong.

ALL:

Let me be wrong.
But also not know it.
Be wrong,
Be wrong,
And, oh, not to know it.
Oh! Let me be wrong.
Oh! Let me be wrong.
Oh! Let me be wrong.
I want to be wrong!

(They repeat the song and walk down the aisles selling Tootsie Tootsies.)

END

LYRIC BY
MARIA IRENE FORNÉS

"THE SUCCESSFUL LIFE OF 3"
SONG TO IGNORANCE

MUSIC BY
SAM POTTLE

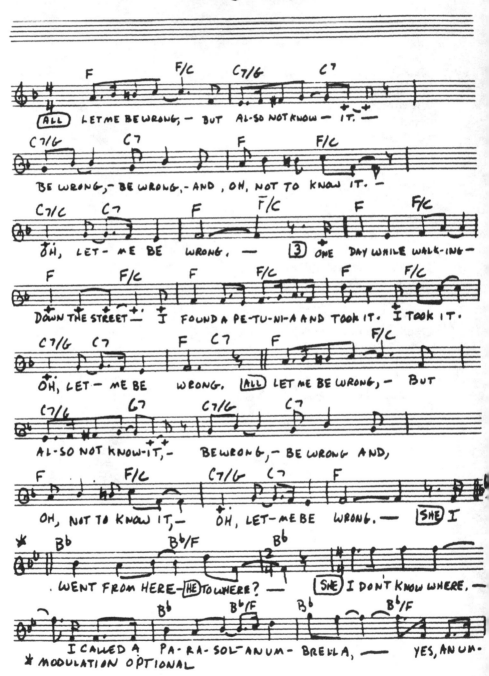

(ALL) LET ME BE WRONG, — BUT AL-SO NOT KNOW — IT. —

BE WRONG, — BE WRONG, — AND, OH, NOT TO KNOW IT. —

OH, LET-ME BE WRONG, — (3) ONE DAY WHILE WALK-ING—

DOWN THE STREET — I FOUND A PE-TU-NI-A AND TOOK IT. I TOOK IT.

OH, LET-ME BE WRONG. (ALL) LET ME BE WRONG, — BUT

AL-SO NOT KNOW-IT, — BE WRONG, — BE WRONG AND,

OH, NOT TO KNOW IT, — OH, LET-ME BE WRONG. — (SHE) I

WENT FROM HERE — (HE) TO WHERE? — (SHE) I DON'T KNOW WHERE, —

I CALLED A PA-RA-SOL-AN UM-BRELLA, — YES, AN UM-

* MODULATION OPTIONAL

OH, LET—ME BE WRONG.—   OH, LET—ME BE WRONG.

OH, LET—ME BE   WRONG, BE WRONG,—

I WANT—TO BE   WRONG.

D.S. (f.) FOR PLAYOFF

Tango Palace

To the memory of my father
Carlos Fornes 1891-1945

Tango Palace was first presented by the San Francisco Actors Workshop at the Encore Theatre in San Francisco on November 29, 1963, under the title *There! You Died*. It was directed by Herbert Blau, with scene design and costumes by Judith Davis, lighting by Dan Dugan, and the following cast:

Isidore:	*Robert Benson*
Leopold:	*Dan Sullivan*

CHARACTERS:

Isidore, an androgynous clown
Leopold, an earnest youth

SCENE:

A room, the same throughout the play. The floor is carpeted. The door is bolted with an oversize padlock. There is a big filing cabinet, an armchair, a secretary, a wall mirror, a water jug, a radio, three porcelain teapots, a large vase, a blackboard. There is a large canvas sack on the floor. A recess in the back wall serves as a shrine. Within the recess, hanging from nails, are a guitar, a whip, a toy parrot, a Persian helmet, two swords, a cape, a compass, a muleta, a pair of bulls horns, six banderillas, two masks in the form of beetles' faces. The shrine is decorated with a string of flower-shaped lightbulbs. Isidore sits in the shrine. His appearance is a mixture of man and woman. He is stout, has long hair, and is wearing rouge and lipstick; he wears a man's hat and pants, high-heeled shoes, and a silk blouse. There is a corsage of flowers pinned on his shirt. Sometimes his behavior is clearly masculine; other times he could be thought a woman. Leopold is inside the canvas sack. He is in his twenties. He is handsome, and his movements are simple. He wears a business suit. Each time Isidore feels he has said something important, he takes a card from his pocket or from a drawer and flips it across the room in any direction. (The word "card" in the script indicates when a card should be flipped.) This action is automatic.

SCENE 1

(*Isidore makes a gesture and his shrine is lit. He makes another gesture and chimes sound. One more gesture and the bulbs on his shrine light up. Leopold begins to move inside the canvas sack. Isidore notices the sack and cautiously approaches it.*)

ISIDORE: Look what the stork has brought me.

(*Isidore opens the sack. Leopold begins to emerge. They stare at each other for a while. Isidore is delighted with what he has found. He goes to the shrine, takes the guitar and begins to sing "A Sleepy Lagoon" in an attempt to charm Leopold.*)

Song and guitar accompaniment by Isidore. (*Card.*)

(*Leopold has gotten out of the sack and walks curiously about the room. He stops in front of the armchair. Isidore, noticing Leopold's interest in the furniture, addresses him in the affected tones of a salesman in an exclusive shop.*)

Queen Anne walnut armchair. Representing the acme of artistic craftsmanship of the Philadelphia school. Circa 1740. Original condition and finish. (*Card.*)

(*Isidore steps down from the shrine, walks ostentatiously past Leopold, and runs his hand along the surface of the secretary.*)

Very rare, small, Louis-Quinze secretary, representing the acme of artistic craftsmanship of the Parisian school. A pure Louis-Quinze leg was never, under any conditions, straight. It was always curvilinear, generally in that shaping which we have come to know as the "cabriole." (*Card. Taking little steps to the mirror.*) Louis-Quatorze carved and gilded mirror. (*Card.*) Bearing sprays of leafage and flowers. Circa 1700. Height sixty-four inches. Width thirty-six inches.

(*Isidore walks close to Leopold and looks him over.*)

The choice of the examples here is influenced by their significance as distinct types representative of the best tradition, not only in the style and execution but in the choice of subject. (*Card. Isidore walks toward the shelf containing the porcelain objects.*) Teapots of rarest Chinese export porcelain with American marine decoration. Circa 1840-1850. Left one shows American Flag, right one American admiral's insignia. The one in the center depicts the so-called "Governor Duff," actually Diedrick Durven, Governor-general of the Dutch East India Company. Exquisite, isn't it? This collection has been formed throughout a period of many years, and it is probably not an exaggeration to say that such a collection could not be formed again. (*Waiting for a reaction.*) Did you say something? . . . Oh, well . . . Listen . . . Music . . . A tango . . . (*Card. Isidore begins to dance.*) Do you know this step? Stomach in. Derriere out. Fingers gracefully curved. (*Card.*) A smile on your lips. Eyes full of stars. Dancing has well been called the poetry of motion. It is the art whereby the feelings of the mind are expressed by measured steps, regulated motions of the body, and graceful gestures. The German waltz, the Spanish fandango, the Polish mazurka, and last but not least the Argentine tango. One . . . two . . . three . . . dip and turn your head to show your profile. One . . . two . . . three . . . dip and swing your little foot back and forth. (*Leopold begins to imitate Isidore.*) One . . . two . . . three . . . and rotate on one foot, taking little steps with the other. Watch me first. Now you made me lose my step. And a one and a two and a three. Stomach in. Derriere out. Fingers gracefully curved. A smile on your lips. Eyes full of stars. One . . . two . . . three . . . dip and profile. One . . . two . . . three . . . and rotate. (*Leopold's attention is drawn by the shrine; he moves closer to it.*) Don't look there yet. Watch me . . . watch me. (*Leopold watches for a moment, then he turns to the shrine again and reaches for the whip. Isidore takes the whip and demonstrates its use.*) This is my whip. (*Lashing Leopold.*) And that is pain. (*Card.*) A souvenir of love. I loved her. She loved me. I gave her the whip. She gave me her cherry . . . All is fair in love and war. (*Card. Taking the parrot.*) This is my talking parrot. (*To the parrot.*) Pretty parrot. (*Speaking in a parrot voice.*) Pretty parrot. (*In his own voice.*) Very smart. He knows everything. (*In a parrot voice.*) Very smart. He knows everything. (*In his own voice.*) Thank you. (*In a *parrot voice.*) Thank you. (*Putting on the Persian helmet.*) And this is the genuine Persian helmet I wore when I fought at Salamis. (*Card.*) I killed two hundred and fifteen Athenians. Fourteen were captains, three were generals, and the rest foot soldiers. I'll show you. (*Isidore takes the sword and swings it while he screams, grunts, whirls, and hops. Leopold becomes frightened.*) That's how I killed them. Don't be afraid, I won't hurt you. (*Touching Leopold's chest with the tip of the sword.*) Do you have something to show me?

LEOPOLD: No. I don't have anything.

ISIDORE: Nothing at all?

LEOPOLD: No.

ISIDORE: Oh, that's too bad. Here, I'll show you my flying cape. (*Isidore puts on the cape, climbs on a chair, flips his arms, and jumps to the floor.*) Extraordinary, isn't it? Would you like to see my joy compass? (*Showing him the joy compass.*) It's magic. I sent for it . . . it points to joy. Now you show me something.

LEOPOLD: I don't own anything.

ISIDORE: Were your things taken away?

LEOPOLD: No, I never had anything, except . . .

ISIDORE: What?

LEOPOLD: A tattoo. (*He opens his shirt.*)

ISIDORE: Oh, how beautiful. (*Reading.*) "This is man. Heaven or bust." Oh, that's in bad taste. That's in terrible taste. (*Card.*) Just for that you can't touch any of my things. The only things you can touch are those cards. Those cards are yours. (*Card.*)

LEOPOLD: (*Picking up a card.*) These cards are mine? (*Reading.*) "A tattoo." "Oh. How beautiful. This is man. Heaven or bust. Oh, that's in bad taste."

ISIDORE: You can put them there in that filing cabinet.

LEOPOLD: (*Disturbed.*) Why do you write what I say?

ISIDORE: First of all, I write what *we* say. And then I don't write. I print . . . with my magic printing press . . . if you'd like to know. File them in your filing cabinet. That cabinet is yours too.

LEOPOLD: What for?

ISIDORE: So you can find them when you need them. These cards contain wisdom. File them away. (*Card.*) Know where they are. (*Card.*) Have them at hand. (*Card.*) Be one upon whom nothing is lost. (*Card.*) Memorize them and you'll be where you were. (*Card.*) Be where you are. Then and now. Pick them up.

LEOPOLD: (*Reading a card.*) "All is fair in love and war."

ISIDORE: That's a good one.

LEOPOLD: Why?

ISIDORE: Because it teaches you that all is fair in love and war, and it teaches you that when someone is telling you a story about love and war, you are not to stand there and say . . . That's not fair . . . or you'll be considered a perfect fool. (*Card.*)

LEOPOLD: (*Still disturbed.*) I don't see why love in war should be different from love in anything else.

ISIDORE: (*Pulling Leopold's ear and shouting.*) Not love *in* war. Love *and* war! It has taken centuries . . . (*Smack.*) Centuries, to arrive at this ethical insight *and you say it isn't fair.* (*Smack.*) All is fair. You hear? All is fair in love . . . (*smack*) and war. (*Smack.*)

LEOPOLD: I don't want your cards. I don't want to have anything to do with them.

ISIDORE: These are not my cards. They are yours. It's you who need learning, not me. I've learned already. (*Card.*) I know all my cards by heart. (*Card.*) I can recite them in chronological order and I don't leave one word out. (*Card.*) What's more I never say a thing which is not an exact quotation from one of my cards. (*Card.*) That's why I never hesitate. (*Card.*) Why I'm never short of an answer. (*Card.*) Or a question. (*Card.*) Or a remark, if a remark is more appropriate.

LEOPOLD: I don't want to learn that way.

ISIDORE: There is no other way.

LEOPOLD: Yes, there is. I hear a voice.

ISIDORE: What voice? That's me you hear. I am the only voice.

LEOPOLD: No, it's not you.

ISIDORE: It is so. (*In a falsetto voice.*) Listen to me and always obey me . . . It's me . . . me . . . It's me . . . and only me . . . Leopold . . . Lippy . . . *me* . . . *me* . . .

LEOPOLD: No.

ISIDORE: Well, *Dime con quien andas y te dire quien eres* . . . (*Card.*) Spanish proverb meaning . . . You know what it means, and if you don't, go and ask that voice of yours. (*Pause.*) What does your voice say?

LEOPOLD: You speak like a parrot.

ISIDORE: No, I don't. My diction is better. Sally says she sells sea shells at the seashore? Have you ever heard a parrot say: Sally says she sells sea shells at the seashore?

LEOPOLD: That's not what I mean.

ISIDORE: (*Considers for a moment.*) I talk like a wise parrot. Study hard, learn your cards, and one day, you too will be able to talk like a parrot.

LEOPOLD: (*Imitating a parrot.*) Study hard, learn your cards and one day, you too will be able to talk like a parrot.

ISIDORE: What are you, a parrot? Do you want to be a moron for the rest of your life? Always being pushed around? (*Isidore pushes Leopold.*) Are you mentally retarded? Do I have to tell you what should be obvious to a half-wit? (*Smack.*) It should be obvious (*smack*) even (*smack*) to a half-wit. (*Leopold throws a punch at Isidore. Isidore ducks, and kicks Leopold. Leopold falls. Isidore turns and thrusts his buttocks out.*) You bad, bad boy. You'll have to be punished. You tried to hit your loving teacher. Come. (*Isidore picks Leopold up.*)

LEOPOLD: (*Freeing himself from Isidore.*) Take your hands off me. (*Leopold executes each of Isidore's commands at the same time as it is spoken, but as if he were acting spontaneously rather than obeying.*)

ISIDORE: Walk to the door. (*Card.*) Notice the padlock. (*Card.*) Push the door. (*Card.*) You're locked in. (*Card.*) Stand there and think. (*Card.*) Why are you locked in? (*Card.*) Where are you locked in? (*Card.*) Turn to the door. (*Card.*) You know what to do. (*Card.*) Pull the padlock. (*Card.*) Push the door. (*Card.*) Force the padlock. (*Card.*) You are locked in. (*Card.*) Kick the door. (*Card.*) Bang the door. (*Card.*) Scream.

ISIDORE & LEOPOLD: Anybody there! Anybody there! (*Card.*) Let me out. (*Card.*) Open up! (*Card.*)

ISIDORE: Kick the door. (*Card.*) Walk around the room restlessly. (*Card.*) Bite your thumbnail. (*Card.*) Get an idea. (*Card.*) You got an idea. (*Card. Leopold charges toward Isidore.*) Violence does not pay. (*Card.*) Be sensible, stand still a moment being sensible. Have sensible thoughts. For every door there's a key. (*Card.*) The key must be in the room. Look for it in the obvious place first. Under the rare seventeenth-century needlework carpet depicting Elijah in the desert fed by ravens. It's not there. Look in Louis-Quinze secretary, mahogany wood. Look in less obvious places. Magnificent marked Wedgwood vase in Rosso Antico ground. In flyleaf of my Gutenberg Bible. Look in places which are not obvious at all. Correction. All places are obvious places. (*Card.*) Look again in drawer of very rare, small, Louis-Quinze secretary, representing the acme of artistic craftsmanship. Fall exhausted on Queen Anne chair. Have desperate thoughts. (*Leopold kicks the chair. Isidore speaks soothingly, to regain control.*) Collect yourself, darling. You must collect yourself.

LEOPOLD: I must collect myself.

ISIDORE: You must collect yourself. You must think, dear. Let's think. Could you have enemies? Perhaps business associates? Perhaps people who envy you? Or could it be the others? The angry husbands? The spinsters? The barking dogs? The man whose toilet you dirtied?

LEOPOLD: Could it be you?

ISIDORE: Could it be you? It doesn't really matter. You might as well stay. Just tidy up your things, darling. Do as I said. File them away.

LEOPOLD: (*Picks up a card and reads it.*) And that is pain.

ISIDORE: Be where you were. (*Card.*)

LEOPOLD: (*Reading another card.*) Pretty parrot. Very smart. He knows everything.

ISIDORE: Then and now. (*Card.*)

LEOPOLD: (*Reading another card.*) Were your things taken away?

ISIDORE: Nothing is lost. (*Card.*)

LEOPOLD: Nothing is lost?

ISIDORE: Nothing. Come, it's time for your drawing lesson. (*Isidore rings the bell and walks to the blackboard to illustrate the lesson.*) How to draw a portrait. (*Making a mark at the top of the blackboard.*) This is the divine. Cleopatra, for example. (*Making a mark at the bottom of the blackboard.*) This down here is the despicable. The werewolf. Now we're going to place the person whose portrait we're drawing. Where shall we put him? Close to the divine? Not so close. Halfway down? Close to the despicable? No. Here. (*Isidore makes a mark to the left and halfway between the other two marks.*) Now you join the points with lines. This is the portrait of a mediocre person. (*Doing it.*) You can draw a mouth on it. And an eye. But it isn't necessary. Because what counts is the nose.

(*The figure Isidore has drawn looks like this:*)

LEOPOLD: Draw my portrait.

ISIDORE: Unfortunately this system doesn't do you any good, since all we can establish is that I am at the top. And way down at the bottom is you. There is no other point. We therefore can't have an angle. We have only a vertical line. The space around us is infinite, enclosed as it may be, because there is not a third person. And if the space around us is infinite, so is, necessarily, the space between us.

LEOPOLD: Who says you're at the top?

ISIDORE: I.

LEOPOLD: I say you're not at the top.

ISIDORE: But I am.

LEOPOLD: How do you know?

ISIDORE: Because I know everything. I know my cards. I know everything.

LEOPOLD: I'm going to burn those cards.

ISIDORE: You'll die if you burn them . . . don't take my word for it. Try it. (*Leopold sets fire to a card.*) What in the world are you doing? Are you crazy? (*Isidore puts the fire out.*) Are you out of your mind? You're going to die. Are you dying? Do you feel awful? (*Isidore trips Leopold.*) There! You died.

LEOPOLD: (*Springing to his feet.*) No, I tripped. I think I tripped.

ISIDORE: See? You tripped because you burned that card. If I hadn't put the fire out you would have died.

LEOPOLD: I don't believe you.

ISIDORE: You don't believe me? You could have broken your neck. All right, I don't care what you think. You just stop burning things.

LEOPOLD: You're lying to me, aren't you?

ISIDORE: Go on, burn them if you want to. I won't stop you. (*Leopold moves to burn a card but then stops himself. Isidore flips a card at Leopold.*) Wisdom. (*Card. Isidore begins to dance.*)

LEOPOLD: (*Holding Isidore to stop him from dancing.*) I beg you.

ISIDORE: Don't put your hands on me, ever, ever, ever, ari, ari, ari. That's Bengali, you know. (*Card.*) It's you who need learning. (*Card.*) Very smart. He knows everything. (*Card.*) A souvenir of love. She gave me her cherry. (*Card.*) I killed two hundred and fifteen Athenians. (*Card.*) That's a good one. (*Card.*) A sleepy lagoon. (*Card.*) What does your voice say? (*Card.*)

LEOPOLD: Stop flipping those things at me . . . I beg you . . . Don't . . . Please . . . I beg you. (*Kneels at Isidore's feet.*)

ISIDORE: And a one and a two. One, two, three, dip and turn . . . You still have to be punished. Don't think I forgot. (*Isidore takes Leopold by the hand and walks him to a corner. Leopold leans against the wall.*) Straighten yourself up. Are you hearing things again? I'm jealous. I want to hear too. (*Putting his ear against Leopold's ear.*) Where is it? I can't hear a thing. (*Talking into Leopold's ear.*) Yoo hoo. Where are you? Say something. Talk to me. It won't talk to me. (*To Leopold.*) Tell me what it says. I'm angry. (*Isidore sits on the shrine, crosses his legs and his arms, and turns his head away from Leopold.*) I'm angry. Don't talk to me. I said don't talk to me. Don't you see I'm in the typical position of anger? . . . Do you want to say something to me?

LEOPOLD: No.

ISIDORE: Well, I want you to tell me what that awful voice was telling you.

LEOPOLD: It said, "Isidore deceives you." It said, "Don't listen to Isidore."

ISIDORE: Oh. Horrible. Horrible. Treason in my own house.

LEOPOLD: Let me tell you . . .

ISIDORE: Oh. Don't say any more, treason. Oh.

LEOPOLD: Let me tell you what I think, Isidore.

ISIDORE: No.

LEOPOLD: Please.

ISIDORE: You've said enough.

LEOPOLD: I haven't said . . .

ISIDORE: Treason!

LEOPOLD: Isidore!

ISIDORE: (*In a whisper.*) Don't talk so loud.

LEOPOLD: (*In a whisper.*) I haven't said . . .

ISIDORE: I heard you already. Treason!

LEOPOLD: I want to leave.

ISIDORE: Bye, bye, butterfly.

LEOPOLD: I want to get out.

ISIDORE: See you later, alligator.

LEOPOLD: Give me the key.

ISIDORE: Pretty parrot.

LEOPOLD: I want the key.

ISIDORE: He wants the key.

PARROT: He wants the key.

ISIDORE: There is no key.

PARROT: No key.

LEOPOLD: You're lying.

ISIDORE: I always tell the truth. I worship truth and truth worships me. Don't be so stubborn. There is no key.

LEOPOLD: There must be a key.

ISIDORE: I see what possesses you. It's faith!

LEOPOLD: So what?

ISIDORE: Faith is a disgusting thing. It's treacherous and destructive. Mountains are moved from place to place. You can't find them. I won't have any of that.

LEOPOLD: Well, I do have faith.

ISIDORE: Infidel. I'm too upset. I can't take any more of this. (*Covers his face.*) It's the devil. I can't look at you. Tell me you'll give it up. Tell me you have no faith.

LEOPOLD: But I do.

ISIDORE: Well, I'm a mountain. *Move me.*

LEOPOLD: I know there is a way out because there have been moments I have been away from here.

ISIDORE: That's not true. You get ten demerits for telling lies.

LEOPOLD: It is true. There are moments when you have just vanished . . .

ISIDORE: Vanished? I have never vanished.

LEOPOLD: I don't mean vanished . . . exactly . . . I mean there are moments when I've felt this is not all there is.

ISIDORE: What else is there?

LEOPOLD: Close your eyes . . . Imagine . . . that all is calm.

ISIDORE: I don't like playing childish games. I'm supposed to sit there imagining a field of orange blossoms and then you're going to pour a bucket of water on my head. Let me tell you, young man, that I played that game when I was five. Let me tell you that it was I who invented that game. And let me tell you that I didn't invent it to sit there like a fool and get the water on *my* head. I invented it to pour the water on the fool's head. Let me tell you that. You're not smart enough . . . not for old Izzy. (*Card.*)

LEOPOLD: I wasn't going to throw water on you.

ISIDORE: You weren't? Hm . . . all right. Go on.

LEOPOLD: Don't imagine anything in particular. Don't imagine orange groves or anything. Make your mind a blank. Just imagine that you are in perfect harmony with everything around you . . .

ISIDORE: Wait, I have to erase the orange grove.

LEOPOLD: Forget about the orange grove.

ISIDORE: I can't forget the orange grove. It's planted in my mind. I have to uproot it. You put things in my mind and then it's I who have to get rid of them. At least leave me in peace for a moment, while I do the work.

LEOPOLD: I didn't put anything in your mind.

ISIDORE: You said, "Don't think of an orange grove." You did, didn't you?

LEOPOLD: Yes . . .

ISIDORE: Well, the moment you said that, an orange grove popped into my head. Now give me time while I get rid of it. (*Isidore moves about the room as if he were picking up oranges and throwing them over a fence with his eyes closed. Leopold's impatience increases.*) First I'll throw this orange over the fence. Then, this little orange. Then, this orange orange. Now this rotten orange. Now I pull this whole branch off the tree. Oh, oh, it's so hard. Now I pull this orange off the tree. Oh, oh, there are so many. There are thousands and thousands and I think millions and trillions. Oh, I'm tired. No, no, I must not rest. I can't take a moment's rest until I clear away all this mess of oranges. Thousands and thousands of acres, and then I have to clear the other side of the fence, and then the other, and then the other and then dismantle the fence, and then the other fence, and then . . . (*Leopold reaches for the pitcher of water and empties it on Isidore. They remain motionless for a moment. Isidore goes to his shrine and sits in his typical angry position. Leopold walks to the opposite end of the room and sits down.*) I'll never trust you again.

(*The lights fade. Isidore laughs out loud as the curtain falls.*)

SCENE 2

(*The curtain rises with Isidore and Leopold in the same position as at the end of the first scene.*)

ISIDORE: (*Sings.*)
Isidore, I beg you
Have you no heart?
You play games,
And I'm so earnest.
Isidore, I beg you.
Can't you see
You're breaking my heart?
'Cause while I'm so earnest,
You're still playing games.

Sung and composed by Isidore. Sixteen years old. (*Card.*)

(*Leopold looks at Isidore.*) Stop looking at me like that.

LEOPOLD: Like what?

ISIDORE: (*Accompanying himself on the guitar.*) Like a lover. Transfigured by the presence of the beloved. Looking as though you want to breathe the minute bubbles of air imprisoned in each of my pores. (*Card.*) Or like a drug addict who imagines specks of heroin concealed in those beloved dimples. (*Card.*)

LEOPOLD: And you think that's how I'm looking at you, you slob?

ISIDORE: I'm offended. (*Pause.*) Come and make up with old Isidore.

LEOPOLD: Leave me alone.

ISIDORE: You'd die of boredom if I left you alone . . . (*Pause.*) You'd have to come to me sooner or later. Come now. (*Pause.*) What if I don't take you later?

LEOPOLD: The better for me.

ISIDORE: I'll count up to ten.

LEOPOLD: Count up to ten.

ISIDORE: Don't be a stubborn brat.

LEOPOLD: Leave me alone.

ISIDORE: (*Takes the Persian helmet and sets it on Leopold's head.*) I'll let you wear it for a while. There's my baby. Isn't he cute. (*Leopold takes the helmet off.*) See how contradictory you are? When I wouldn't lend it to you, you wanted it. Now that I'm willing to lend it to you, you don't want it.

LEOPOLD: Oh, go to hell. You twist everything.

ISIDORE: Now you're being rude.

LEOPOLD: Go back to your hole. (*Leopold picks up some cards and begins to sort them.*)

ISIDORE: My hole. My hole? (*Isidore looks through his cards.*) He means my shrine. I think I will. (*Isidore goes to the shrine doing a dance step.*) Peekaboo. (*Leopold stands in front of Isidore.*)

LEOPOLD: Listen to me.

ISIDORE: Yes.

LEOPOLD: You're going to start behaving from now on. (*Isidore nods in consent.*) OK. That's all. (*Leopold goes back to the cards. Isidore passes wind through his lips.*)

ISIDORE: So I'm going to start behaving from now on. Then what? . . . Stop being silly. What is the matter with you, young man? You should be ashamed of yourself. What is life without humor here and there? A little bit of humor . . . Look at him sorting out his little cards. He's a good boy.

LEOPOLD: I'm not sorting them. I just don't want to listen to you.

ISIDORE: You can't tear yourself away from them. Can you? . . . You think I haven't seen you running to your cards the moment you think I'm not looking?

LEOPOLD: That's a lie. I've never . . .

ISIDORE: I never lie. I have never lied in my life. (*Card. Isidore crosses himself, then covers his head as if to protect himself from lightning.*) So what if I'm a liar. Do you think truth matters? Well, it doesn't. (*Card.*) Does that confound your infantile mind? It is order that matters, whether there's order or disorder. (*Card.*) A sloppy liar is despicable (*card*), as despicable as a sloppy truth-teller. (*Card.*) Now, what do you deduce from that?

LEOPOLD: That you're rotten. (*Leopold flips a card to Isidore. Isidore sniffs himself.*)

ISIDORE: A systematic liar, a man with a goal, a man with a style is the best sort. (*Card.*) The most reliable. You'll never amount to anything until you learn that. No, you'll never amount to anything. You'll never make it in the army, the navy, politics, business, stardom. You're worthless. I'm almost tempted to give you the key.

LEOPOLD: Give it to me.

ISIDORE: Never mind that. Come here. I'm about to forgive you . . . Come now. You really don't want me to forgive you?

LEOPOLD: Where is it, Isidore?

ISIDORE: Oh, here, in my heart.

LEOPOLD: Where is it?

ISIDORE: Oh, you're so insistent. I'll tell you what. (*Isidore takes the horns and the cape.*) I'll answer all the questions you want if you do a little thing for me. Be a good bull and charge. Then I'll answer your question.

LEOPOLD: You'll tell me where the key is?

ISIDORE: Yes. Charge six times and I'll give you the key . . . But you won't be satisfied with the key. On the contrary, it's when you have the key that you'll start asking questions. You'll start wondering about the mysteries of the universe. (*Counting the banderillas.*) One, two, three, four, five, six mysteries has the universe. As I stick each banderilla in your back I'll reveal the answer to a mystery. And then (*taking the sword*) the moment of truth. Right through the back of your neck. Oh, beautiful transgressions. While I'm answering your last question you'll be expiring your last breath. As eternal verity is revealed to you, darkness will come upon your eyes . . . Fair? Fair. Charge.

LEOPOLD: Are you kidding?

ISIDORE: I am not kidding. I am proposing the most poetic diversion ever enjoyed by man. You mean to say you're not willing to die for the truth? (*Isidore rubs his fingers to indicate "shame."*)

LEOPOLD: And when I'm crawling and bleeding to death begging you to answer my questions you'll say something like . . . Ha ha.

ISIDORE: You want to play or you don't want to play?

LEOPOLD: I'll play. But I'll only charge six times. Six passes. I only want one answer. No mysteries.

ISIDORE: All right. Ask your question.

LEOPOLD: Where is the key?

ISIDORE: Charge.

LEOPOLD: Answer first.

ISIDORE: The answer after you charge. (*Leopold begins to charge.*) Wait. I lost the mood. I need preparation. (*Isidore kneels in front of the shrine and crosses himself. He makes a trumpet with his hand and toots a bullfighter's march. Isidore performs the passes as he calls out the passes' names.*) Toro and bull. Fearless, confident and dominant, without altering the composure of his figure. Isidore lifts the spectators from their seats as he receives his enemy with *Veronica.*

LEOPOLD: One.

ISIDORE: (*Turns his back toward the audience.*) Turning his back to the planks below the box occupied by the Isidore Fan Club to whom he has dedicated this bull. He performs a dangerous *Revolera.* Marvelous both in its planning and development.

LEOPOLD: Two.

ISIDORE: *Faroles.* And the embellishment.

LEOPOLD: Four.

ISIDORE: Three. A punishing pass. *Pase de castigo.* All of Isidore's passes have identical depth and majestic sobriety.

LEOPOLD: Four.

ISIDORE: *Manoletina.* Astounding elegance and smoothness. The music breaks out and competes with the deafening clamor of the multitude.

LEOPOLD: Five. (*Isidore bows, Leopold charges.*)

ISIDORE: Then, with authentic domination, he performs the *Isidorina.* (*Isidore circles the stage and bows.*) Ovation. One ear, turn. And cheers.

LEOPOLD: Six. Answer.

ISIDORE: Gore me.

LEOPOLD: Answer.

ISIDORE: Gore me. That's the answer. (*Leopold charges against Isidore, this time determined to get him. Isidore avoids him with a banderillo's turn while he thrusts a banderilla into Leopold's back.*) Saint Sebastian! (*Leopold falls to the floor. Isidore kneels beside him and holds him in his arms.*) Good bull. He attacked nobly and bravely. His killer made him take fifty-one passes and he would have continued charging, following docilely the course marked by deceit. He was cheered as he was hauled out, but less than he deserved. (*Isidore pulls out the banderilla from Leopold's back and caresses him tenderly. Leopold looks at Isidore imploringly. Isidore kisses Leopold.*) I have no alternative.

LEOPOLD: Don't tell me that, Isidore. I can't believe that.

ISIDORE: I have no alternative, Leopold.

LEOPOLD: No alternative? The alternative is simple.

ISIDORE: It isn't simple. I can't be good to you.

LEOPOLD: Just try.

ISIDORE: It's not within my power.

LEOPOLD: Have you no will then?

ISIDORE: No, I don't will it.

LEOPOLD: Who wills it?

ISIDORE: You, Leopold.

LEOPOLD: Me? It is not me, Isidore. You can't be right.

ISIDORE: It is you, Leopold.

LEOPOLD: I have never provoked you. I have never wished for anything but kindness from you. I have never tried but for your love.

ISIDORE: Yes, and maybe it is just that. Maybe you have been too patient, too good-natured. (*Leopold is astounded. There is a moment's pause. He then struggles with Isidore to break from his embrace.*)

LEOPOLD: You are rotten . . . What are you? What are you that you must have rottenness around you? I am too patient? Too good-natured? I will not become rotten for you. I will not become rotten for you. (*Leopold holds Isidore by the neck and tries to strangle him.*)

ISIDORE: (*Gasping for air.*) Son . . . son . . . let me tell you . . . let me tell you . . . a story . . . There was once a man . . . who . . . (*Leopold covers his ears.*) It's very important. You must listen. There was once a man whose only companion was a white rat. He loved this white rat dearly. And one day the rat disappeared. The rat couldn't have left the room, because there were no doors, or windows, or even cracks on the walls or floor. Then the man, thinking that the rat could have hidden in some nook or cranny unknown to him, took his axe and wrecked everything he owned . . . The rat was nowhere in his room. He then turned to a picture of the rat which was hanging on the wall, and was about to wield his axe against it . . . but he stopped himself . . . He said, "This is the only thing I have left of my rat. If I destroy the picture, I will have nothing left to remind me of him." And from that moment on, he began to speak to the picture of the rat and to caress it, and even feed it. Eventually, though, his loneliness brought him to such a state of melancholia that he no longer cared whether he was happy or not. He did not even care whether he lived or died. And as if he were summoning his own death, he picked up his axe and smashed the picture of the rat. There, trapped in the wires that supported the picture, was his beloved rat, who had died of starvation. The dead rat turned his head to face the man and said (*as if imitating a ghost*), "If you had not been satisfied with my picture you could have had me. You chicken-hearted bastard," and then disintegrated into dust.

LEOPOLD: (*Frightened.*) A fairy tale.

ISIDORE: There is a moral to it, Leopold. Try to understand it.

LEOPOLD: The dead don't speak.

ISIDORE: Yes, they do. You'll see, you'll see. Understand the story, Leopold. You must relinquish what you want or you will never have it.

LEOPOLD: I understand one thing. There is something that moves you. There is something that makes you tender and loving, only one thing: nastiness . . . and meanness and abuse.

ISIDORE: Those are three things, Leopold.

LEOPOLD: They're all the same.

ISIDORE: It's our fate.

LEOPOLD: Not mine . . . I love . . .

ISIDORE: You don't love. Don't you see that. All you do is whine!

LEOPOLD: It's time you answered my question, Isidore.

ISIDORE: I answered it.

LEOPOLD: You told me to gore you.

ISIDORE: Yes, I did.

LEOPOLD: Is that the answer?

ISIDORE: That was my answer.

LEOPOLD: You stabbed me. I want my answer.

ISIDORE: There is a way, Leopold, but only one. You must find it yourself.

LEOPOLD: That's no answer. You wounded me.

ISIDORE: You tried to gore me. I had to defend myself.

LEOPOLD: You told me to gore you.

ISIDORE: That was part of the game.

LEOPOLD: Stinking bastard. Can you bear your own rottenness? You must atone for your wickedness sometime. You cannot go on without a purge. Do you ever pray? Do you beat your fist against your chest and ask for forgiveness? If not to redeem yourself, at least to be able to go on with your viciousness. You could not endure it without a purge. Do you spend your nights covering your ears to keep away the sound of my moans? Do you cry then? . . . Could it be that you do it out of stupidity, that you don't know the difference between right and wrong? Oh no. Let it be anything but that. Let it be malice. If you do it out of a decision to be harmful, I can convince you that it's best to be good. But if you don't know the difference between right and wrong, is there anything I can do? Maybe you must be vicious in spite of yourself. Maybe you have to do it . . . to protect me from something worse? . . . for my own good? (*Leopold throws himself on his knees with his head on Isidore's lap.*) Give me a sign, a smile, a look. Tell me you love me. (*Isidore pouts innocently. He makes a circle with his arm and places his hand on Leopold's head. The lights fade.*)

SCENE 3

(*Isidore and Leopold are in the same position. Isidore stretches himself and yawns. He jerks his thighs slightly to make Leopold's head roll and fall to the floor. Isidore looks at Leopold who is waking up and smiles. Isidore stands up, stretches again, and does a dance step.*)

ISIDORE: Cheery-uppy, Leopold. (*The following scene is to have a nightmarish quality. Isidore and Leopold dance in a ritualistic manner. Isidore puts on one of*

the two beetle masks, the one which is wingless, and gives the other to Leopold.
Leopold should behave like a sleep-walker.) Beetles are versatile little animals.
For great numbers, the end of autumn does not mean the end of their lives.
There are more beetles by far than any other kind of insect. Over a quarter
of a million beetle species have been described. Beetles are in constant conflict with man because there are few of the organic commodities that man
has learned to use that do not also interest some beetle. Some spend their
life in the thick flesh of century-plant leaves and when caught make an excellent salad, tasting something like a shrimp salad. Other notable varieties
are: The Clavicornia, the segments of whose torso are variable in number
and whose antennae are equipped with a more or less (*Isidore does a bump*
and grind) distinct club, the terminal segments being broader than the
others. The Hydrophilidae (*Isidore places his arms in arabesque position*)
Silphidae, Staphylinidae, Nitidulidae (*convulsing*), Histeridae, Coccinellidae,
Ebonychisae (*holding his breasts*), Erotylidae, Languiridae, and Dermestidae.
The literature of beetles is enormous.

LEOPOLD: (*Crawling on the floor.*) When things are in disorder and I move, I
feel like I'm crawling. As if with every movement I have to drag along with
me the things that are in disorder. As if I had grown brooms on my sides
that extend as far as the wall, to sweep the junk . . . the dust. (*Leopold picks*
up some of the cards, looks at Isidore and smiles sadly.)

ISIDORE: They are for your own good. Ingrate. Don't you know? Come, do me
a pretty beetle.

LEOPOLD: Dirt, my dear sir, comes to us from everywhere. And it comes out
from within us. It comes out through each pore. Then we wash it away, we
flush it away, we drown it, we bury it, we incinerate it, and then we perfume
ourselves. We put odors in our toilets, medicinal odors, terrible odors, but
all these odors seem sweet next to our own. What I want, sir, is to live with
that loathsome mess near me, not to flush it away. To live with it for all
those who throw perfume on it. To be so dirty for those who want to be so
clean. To do them that favor. I wanted to drop it in the pot and leave it
there for days, and live with it.

ISIDORE: Sometimes you touch the realm of romance.

LEOPOLD: In the latter part of the afternoon I feel cold, I feel the stuff in my
bowels. And I feel downcast. The open air is in my mind, but my eyes
wander around this cave. I feel such pain for being here.

ISIDORE: The contrast between your poet's taste for languid amusement and
my unconventional pageantry sends such fresh impetus throbbing through
my veins.

LEOPOLD: I see a light in you. The only light. I see it through a tunnel lower
than myself. Attempting to go through it and hoping to be invited, I crawl.

ISIDORE: Crawl then. Crawl then. (*Leopold crawls.*)

LEOPOLD: I liked to think I was an exception, of course, I pretended I was not one more snake. And to prove I was an exception, I tried to stand erect, and to stand erect I needed you to support me, and when you refused I had to beg, and to beg I had to crawl, and snakes crawl, and I am a snake. When crawling tires me, I stand erect. It is to exhaustion and disillusion that I owe my dignity. Not to pride . . . Oh . . . I cannot make your eyes turn to me with love.

ISIDORE: Give me a pretty smile, pretty beetle. (*Leopold opens his mouth wide.*)

LEOPOLD: To make dirt come out through the mouth you have to close your holes very tight, and let the dirt rot inside. Then it will come out through any opening.

ISIDORE: The prophet, the prophet. Come and hear the dirty prophet.

LEOPOLD: (*Taking off his mask.*) Oh, Isidore, you are my enemy.

ISIDORE: I am not your enemy.

LEOPOLD: Come here. Let me see you. (*Isidore moves near Leopold.*) Take that mask off. (*Isidore takes the mask off.*) You *are* my enemy.

ISIDORE: What makes you say that?

LEOPOLD: Your smell . . .

ISIDORE: How do I smell?

LEOPOLD: You stink.

ISIDORE: Not true. What you smell is your own stink. You are putrid.

LEOPOLD: I'm going to kill you.

ISIDORE: Don't, you're trying to scare me. You're trying to scare me so I'll be good to you.

LEOPOLD: No . . . I know nothing can make you change. No . . . If I were to frighten you you'd behave for a while, but then you would get to like it, and you'd want more and more of it.

ISIDORE: And you wouldn't do it just to please your old friend?

LEOPOLD: No, I wouldn't. I have already played too many of your games. I have become as corrupt as you intended me to be. But . . . no more.

ISIDORE: You can't stop now. It's too late.

LEOPOLD: I know. That's why I've decided to kill you.

ISIDORE: You have? (*Leopold goes to the shrine and gets the knife. Isidore hides behind a piece of furniture and begins a mock trembling.*)

LEOPOLD: Get up, Isidore.

ISIDORE: No. (*Leopold lifts the knife and holds it up for a moment, then lowers it slowly.*)

LEOPOLD: If I killed you what would I be?

ISIDORE: A murderer . . . that's what you'd be . . . a murderer. A dirty ratty murderer.

LEOPOLD: There will be no one to judge me.

ISIDORE: Yourself . . . you'll judge yourself. You'll die of guilt.

LEOPOLD: Guilt? Is that what it is?

ISIDORE: Yes. And then you'll be all alone. You don't know what it is to be alone. It's horribly . . . lonely.

LEOPOLD: I'm afraid of my own death. I see myself dead.

ISIDORE: You're not going to do it then?

LEOPOLD: You're disappointed.

ISIDORE: Yes, I thought I was going to have some thrills and suspense, never knowing when you would strike . . . having to sleep with one eye open. But as usual you are a party-pooper . . . You could never kill me, Leopold. Don't you see? You are just what I want you to be. You only know what I have taught you. And I haven't taught you how to kill.

LEOPOLD: You have offended me. If you died I still would be offended.

ISIDORE: I have offended you and you haven't challenged me to a duel? Challenge me to a duel immediately . . . What kind of a mouse are you . . . I have offended you. I am offending you right now. You mouse. (Smack.) You mouse. (Smack.) You misbegotten mouse. You misbegotten, lifeless mouse.

LEOPOLD: If I killed you the offense would not be undone. If you died, you would not be able to atone for it.

ISIDORE: Don't worry, there isn't a chance of that. I'll kill you and be done with you. (Isidore puts the sword in Leopold's hand.)

LEOPOLD: If you killed me you would be convinced that you had the right to offend me.

ISIDORE: Beautiful, beautiful. Let's duel. You'll fight for your offended pride. I, for the right to offend you. Come on. Come on.

LEOPOLD: Please stop, Isidore.

ISIDORE: No, this is fun. It's fun. En garde.

LEOPOLD: (Poking different objects with his sword.) What are these things . . . Leopold? Leopold? Are you Leopold? Are you . . . they don't strike back. You are Leopold.

ISIDORE: Too much reflection. (Isidore pokes Leopold with the sword. Leopold shrinks back.)

LEOPOLD: Each time I hold back I die a little.

ISIDORE: That's why you stink, you're putrid with death. Cleanliness is close to godliness. (Card.) I still have a lot to teach you.

LEOPOLD: (Swaying.) I feel faint. If only I could find a spot to fix on and steady myself.

ISIDORE: (Swaying and lurching.) Look at me. Let me be the spot. Look, everything is moving. But I am steady as a rock.

LEOPOLD: Come here, Isidore. Open your arms. (Isidore obeys. Leopold lifts the sword slowly, points it to Isidore's heart, and pushes it into his body. Isidore falls to the floor.)

ISIDORE: How could you do this? (Leopold holds Isidore in his arms. He doesn't answer.) Say you're sorry and my wound will heal.

LEOPOLD: I know.

ISIDORE: Say you're sorry.

LEOPOLD: If I do you'll curse me.

ISIDORE: I beg you, Leopold, I'm dying.

LEOPOLD: Die, Isidore . . . I understand now . . . You made it clear enough . . . (*Isidore dies.*) It is done. All the thought and preparation did not help me do it. It is done. And I don't know what made me do it. The moment came. The only moment when it could be done. It possessed me and I let it take me.

(*The stage darkens. The door opens. The sound of harps is heard outside. There is a blue sky. Isidore appears among the clouds dressed as an angel. He carries stacks of cards. He beckons Leopold to follow him. Leopold picks up a few cards, then the sword, then a few more cards. Isidore shakes his head, and shows Leopold the cards he carries. Leopold walks through the door slowly, but with determination. He is ready for the next stage of their battle.*)

END

Molly's Dream

Molly's Dream was first performed at the New Dramatist's Workshop in New York on December 5, 1968 where it received a workshop production, with the following cast:

Molly:	*Julie Bovasso*
The Young Man:	*Ray Barry*
Mack:	*Jim Cashman*
John:	*Leonard Hicks*
Alberta:	*Crystal Field*
The Hanging Women:	*Carol Gelfand, Kay Carney, Penny Dupont, Margaret Impert, Alice Tweedy*

Designed and directed by the author
Music by Cosmos Savage
Lights by Therese King
Musical accompaniment by David Tice

CHARACTERS:

Molly, late twenties, a waitress.
The Young Man, late twenties, a factory worker.
Jim is played by the same actor as the Young Man but he appears endowed
    with sublime sex appeal.
The Hanging Women, a chorus of five.
Mack, a bartender in his forties.
John, a lean middle-aged cowboy.
Alberta, a twenty-seven-year-old, who refuses to grow.

PART I
Molly and the Hanging Women

(*An old-fashioned saloon typical of warm climates. There are several swinging doors on both sides. Both sides of the saloon lead to streets. Another swinging door on the back wall leads to the kitchen. The counter is alongside the back wall. A trap door on the floor behind the counter leads to the basement. There are fans hanging from the ceiling, potted plants, spittoons, tables, and chairs. There is a wall mirror, and a cage with a bird. On the counter there is a gun, and the two porcelain figures—one in the shape of a woman; the other, Cupid. A top hat hangs from a hat rack.*

The play of lights indicated in the script denotes an important moment in the life of one or another character.

Molly is alone in the tavern. She wears a black satin uniform. She prepares herself a cup of coffee, takes off her shoes, sits down and begins to read to herself from a magazine.)

MOLLY: (*She mumbles*) Rosie was a damn good waitress. She wasn't the kind that would spill any whiskey on the counter. (*She reads out loud*) But when Sam started walking toward her, her hand started shaking, and the whiskey spilled. Sam, her beloved Sam, whom she was even thinking of marrying, had shot at the Sheriff. What a thing to do. This broke her heart and made her nervous. That's why she spilled the drink. Sam, who seemed like such a nice guy, had shot at the Sheriff and now he had the nerve to come into the tavern as if nothing had happened, or at least he had the nerve to come into the tavern. He pulled a chair from one of the tables, turned it toward him and straddled it. He looked at her for a while without saying anything. Then he said, "Are you angry because I shot at the Sheriff?" (*Molly puts the magazine down and takes a puff from her cigarette. She speaks the following dialogue out loud, acting out both characters in the story.*) "Are you angry because I shot at the Sheriff?" (*Sarcastically.*) "Naw, I was getting tired of his face. I wouldn't mind seeing someone else wear that star. What would you like?" (*One of the swinging doors opens slightly. The Young Man puts his head in. Molly does not notice him.*) "Let me have a steak . . . rare . . . And don't bother putting arsenic in the gravy." (*Molly writes in her check pad.*) "Rare, no arsenic." —Oh, boy.

(*Molly notices the Young Man. She is flustered. They look at one another for a moment. He smiles and walks away. Molly begins to feel sleepy. She yawns. She leans her head on the table and falls asleep. A dreamlike atmosphere is suggested by means of lights, smoke, or the lifting of the walls. A swinging door opens. Jim puts his head in. He looks exactly like the Young Man and is played by the same actor.*)

JIM: (*Suspiciously.*) Is there a waiter here?
MOLLY: (*Raising her head.*) Yes.

(*Jim enters. He is dressed in glittering lace. He looks like a prince in a fairy tale. Five women surround him as if they were a floating part of him. These are the Hanging Women. When he is still, they hang on to him gently. He sits at a table. Molly stretches and walks to him. She waits for his order.*)

JIM: Isn't there a waiter here?
MOLLY: Yes, me.
JIM: I mean a man waiter.
MOLLY: No, there's just me.

(*Jim looks at Molly for a moment. Then he stands and walks to the door.*)

JIM: I don't need one more woman. (*As Jim exits, the doors swing. Mack enters with a box of soda bottles, goes behind the counter and disappears behind it. Jim puts his head through the doors again.*) Didn't I just see a man behind the bar?
MOLLY: Yes.
JIM: Where did he go?
MOLLY: He's in the basement.
JIM: Is he coming back?
MOLLY: Mack!
MACK: What?
MOLLY: Are you coming back?
MACK: Yes.

MOLLY: Yes, he is coming back.

(*Jim starts walking toward the table where he sat before.*)

JIM: I thought you said there was no waiter.
MOLLY: He's not a waiter.
JIM: (*Stopping.*) What is he?
MOLLY: Bartender.

(*Jim walks to the bar. A few moments pass. Molly looks at him with curiosity. He tries to avoid her glance. Mack appears behind the bar.*)

JIM: A double rye, please. (*Mack pours a drink. Jim takes the drink to a table.*)
MACK: Boy, that's a man for you. . . . Look at that.

(*Mack exits. Molly sits at Jim's table and looks at the Hanging Women.*)

MOLLY: Who are they? (*Jim drinks his rye in one gulp.*)
JIM: Who? (*Molly points to the Hanging Women.*) Friends.
MOLLY: What's the matter with them?
JIM: Nothing is the matter with them.
MOLLY: Why are they hovering over you like that?
JIM: They like me. (*Molly looks at the Hanging Women.*)
MOLLY: Doesn't it bother you to have them . . . (*She gestures. Jim shakes his head.*)
JIM: A little.
MOLLY: Why don't you tell them to scoot?
JIM: I have.
MOLLY: And?
JIM: They won't go.
MOLLY: (*Waving her hands as if to scare away chickens.*) Shhh . . . Shhh . . . (*The Hanging Women flutter.*)
JIM: Don't do that. . . . You'll hurt their feelings. (*Jim looks for Mack. While his head is turned Molly waves her arms with sweeping movements.*)
MOLLY: Shh . . . Shhh . . . (*The Hanging Women scatter all over the room. They are breathless and in a state of anxiety. The lights flash on and remain strong through the following scene.*) They're off. (*Jim is also breathless and in a state of anxiety.*) What's the matter? (*Jim gasps for air.*) I thought you wanted them off.
HANGING WOMEN: (*Sing*)
Do not collapse just now, world.
Do not collapse just now.
Wait a bit. Wait a bit.

Perhaps I can find my way back.

MOLLY: I thought you wanted them off. (*The Hanging Women start moving toward Jim.*)

JIM:

Oh . . . oh . . . oh . . . oh . . .
The flower of love grew on me,
And she pulled it off.

(*The Hanging Women surround him again. Molly pats them.*)

MOLLY: It's all right now.

JIM:

It grew from my side.
It grew from my legs.
It grew from my arms.
The most beautiful thing grew off me.
The flower of love.
And she pulled it off.

HANGING WOMEN: (*Sing.*)

Oh . . . oh . . . oh . . .

MOLLY: It's all right . . . you're back.

HANGING WOMEN:

It's just that I hear
A little bit of love
Going down the drain.
Glop, glop, glop,
Going down the drain.

JIM:

Oh, God. Oh, God.
She put them back.
But she pulled them off.

MOLLY: Gee whiz. (*The lights go back to normal. Jim looks for Mack.*) What do you want?

JIM: I thought I'd ask him for a drink. But that's all right.

MOLLY: (*Standing.*) Double?

JIM: Don't bother.

MOLLY: It's no bother. That what I'm here for.

JIM: I changed my mind. I don't want a drink. (*Molly sits.*)

MOLLY: Are you broke?

JIM: No.

MOLLY: It's on the house.

JIM: Why? (*Molly stares at Jim and speaks distractedly. He recognizes the look and becomes cautious.*)

MOLLY: Oh, I don't know. I just thought I'd buy you a drink.

JIM: Why?

MOLLY: Why? . . . That's how I felt. . . . I felt like buying you a drink. (*She walks toward Jim.*)

JIM: Oh, God . . . Well, don't buy me a drink. You go on out in there.

MOLLY: Where?

JIM: In the kitchen. Go in the kitchen and do what you have to do. Wash some glasses.

MOLLY: I don't wash the glasses. Mack does that.

JIM: Well . . . read your magazine. . . . Don't come so close.

MOLLY: . . . Why not? (*She is very close to him.*)

JIM: Oh, God. (*Molly throws her arms around Jim's neck and lets herself hang. The lights flash on and off.*) Listen . . . lady . . . excuse me a moment. Hey, miss . . .

MOLLY: (*Still hanging. Almost inaudibly.*) What?

JIM: Do I owe you anything?

MOLLY: I don't know.

JIM: Think about it for a moment.

MOLLY: I can't think now.

JIM: Look, I don't owe you anything. You have to let go. (*Molly returns to her chair.*)

MOLLY: Well, what do you expect. I was curious.

JIM: That's all right. Just don't do it again. (*Mack enters.*)

MACK: . . . That's a man for you.

JIM: Double rye, please. (*Mack pours the drink and exits. Jim starts to stand.*)

MOLLY: I'll get it.

JIM: No, it's all right. I'll get it.

MOLLY: (*Going to the bar.*) I'll get it. It's my job.

JIM: No, it's all right. I'd like to get my own drink if you don't mind.

MOLLY: That's all right. I'm the waitress. (*She reaches for the drink.*)

JIM: It's my drink. I get my own drink if I want to.

MOLLY: You can't get your own drink. I get paid to get the drinks.

JIM: It's my drink. I'm paying for it and I don't want any favors.

MOLLY: It's no favor. It's my job. (*Jim grabs her. They struggle for a moment. She manages to put the drink on the table.*) Just leave me a tip.

JIM: You don't need a tip.

MOLLY: What do I need?

JIM: Love. (*Molly hangs again. Mack enters.*)

MACK: You didn't have to bother. Molly would have brought it to you. Where's Molly? (*Discovering her.*) Molly . . . (*Molly doesn't answer.*) Molly, what are you doing?

MOLLY: I'll be up in a minute.

MACK: What do you mean you'll be up in a minute? Molly . . . what in the world are you doing?

JIM: She'll never let go.

MACK: How do you do it?

JIM: It's a burden.

MACK: I wish I had that burden.

JIM: They weigh a lot.

MACK: Leave them home. You don't know how to handle women.

JIM: I can't leave them home. It would hurt their feelings.

MACK: Hurt their feelings? What's the matter with you. Are you a sissy?

JIM: I don't want to hurt their feelings.

MACK: Hey, Molly, forget it, kid. This guy's a sissy. (*She ignores him.*) Hey, Molly, what's the matter with you? He's a sissy.

MOLLY: Shut up, Mack.

JIM: Bunch of creeps.

MACK: That's the trouble with women. Here's me, a real man. You name it, I have it. There's that creep . . . a sissy. . . . Do they go for me? No. They go for him . . . a sissy. (*Mack starts moving furniture as if to prepare for cleaning the floor.*) A burden he says . . . women a burden . . . wish I had that burden. I could take on a hundred. One right after the other. No problem. A hundred. Bang, bang, bang. Just like that. (*Sings.*)
Bang bang bang bang
Bang
Bang bang bang bang
Bang
Bang
Bang
Bang

(*The Hanging Women surround Mack.*)

MACK & THE HANGING WOMEN:
Bang bang bang bang
Bang bang bang bang
Bang bang bang bang
Bang bang bang bang
Bang bang bang bang
Bang
Bang bang bang bang
Bang
Bang
Bang

Bang bang bang bang
Bang bang bang bang

Bang bang bang bang
Bang bang bang bang
Bang bang bang bang
Bang
Bang bang bang bang
Bang
Bang
Bang

Bang bang bang bang
Bang bang bang bang
Bang bang bang bang
Bang bang bang bang
Bang bang bang bang
Bang
Bang bang bang bang
Bang
Bang
Bang

MACK: (*Spoken.*) But do they go for me? . . . No. (*The Hanging Women put their hands on Mack. He collapses.*)

HANGING WOMEN: Creep! (*The Hanging Women go back to Jim. Mack stands. He turns to the Hanging Women the way a wrestler waits for an attack.*)

MACK: Try again. . . . Come on. . . . Come on. . . . Try again. I can take the lot of you. You yellow-bellied broads.

HANGING WOMEN: Creep!

MACK: Aw, bunch of dumb broads. (*John enters. He wears black dungarees, a black shirt, a cowboy hat, and holsters with guns from his ankles to his armpits.*) Hey, Molly, a customer. (*Molly does not respond.*) Hey, Molly.

MOLLY: What?

MACK: Customer.

MOLLY: Wait a moment.

JIM: Molly . . .

MOLLY: What?

JIM: Are you going to stay? (*Pause.*) Molly, are you going to stay? (*Pause.*) I like you, Molly, but I just can't take on any more. (*He waits a moment.*) Listen, you have to let go.

MOLLY: I don't want to.

JIM: Well, you have to. (*Molly lets go.*) Are your feelings hurt?

MOLLY: (*Hurt.*) No.

JIM: Molly, I can't take on any more. I just can't. I can hardly walk as it is. I can't play baseball. Do you understand what it is not to be able to play baseball? I just can't take on any more. And besides, I don't owe you anything.

MOLLY: Well, I liked it.

JIM: All right then, hang on. What's one more?

MOLLY: Not unless the others leave.

JIM: I can't tell them to leave.

MOLLY: Why not?

JIM: I'm indebted to them.

MOLLY: Why?

JIM: Because . . . they like me.

MOLLY: That's nothing.

JIM: I'm indebted to them.

MOLLY: I can do more than that for a man.

JIM: I know, you're different.

MOLLY: So?

JIM: Molly, I can't.

MOLLY: You said I was different.

JIM: I'm indebted to them. (*Molly dries a tear, starts to walk away. Then turns to the Hanging Women and starts waving her arms.*)

MOLLY: Shhh . . . Shhh . . .

JIM: Mollyyy! Don't!

MOLLY: Creep!

(*The lights flash on and remain strong through the following scene. Molly takes off her apron. She gradually develops a German accent. She begins to behave in a manner resembling Marlene Dietrich.*)

MACK: Molly . . . Customer.

MOLLY: (*To John.*) What do you want? (*John thinks a moment and begins to make a gesture.*) Whiskey, double, very straight, hold the chaser, make it fast. He's dry.

JOHN: Make it a Bloody Mary.

MACK: (*While preparing the drink.*) What was it like?

MOLLY: I can't explain it.

MACK: Try.

MOLLY: It felt right. That's all.

MACK: Come on.

MOLLY: You have to live it. You can't explain it.

MACK: (*Pouring whiskey for Molly.*) It's for you.

MOLLY: (*She drinks it.*) Thanks.

MACK: Now tell me.

MOLLY: What.

MACK: What was it like?

MOLLY: It felt right.

MACK: That doesn't mean anything.

MOLLY: It felt right to be near him.

MACK: That's nothing.

MOLLY: It's everything, you dumb creep. You'd never understand.

MACK: Well, explain it to me.

MOLLY: I can't explain it. Try it yourself.

MACK: What do you think I am?

MOLLY: Forget it then.

MACK: Are you going back?

MOLLY: Never again. (*She walks to John's table with his drink.*)

MACK: Ha ha.

MOLLY: What does that mean? Ha ha.

MACK: He's not so good.

MOLLY: He's good all right. I'm just not going back. (*Molly drinks John's drink. She then goes to the bar and sits on it.*)

MACK: What do you mean by drinking the customer's drink? (*Molly shrugs her shoulders.*) Who do you think you are. (*Mack pours another drink for John. Molly lights a cigarette.*) Here, bring it to him. (*Molly does not respond.*) Hey, Molly! . . . Kid! . . . Bring the customer his drink. (*Molly puffs some smoke. The lights start to shift slowly. Molly will be in a spot.*)

MOLLY: Molly kid was. Are you blind, you creep? Can't you see what life has done to me? Molly kid was. I have just changed my name. (*The music starts.*) No. I'm not breaking into song. The moment is too sad. I'm not going back. Good as he is, my feelings are hurt.

JIM: Molly, come back.

MOLLY: Molly was. I have just changed my name. (*The music plays louder as if to invite her to sing.*) No. Little Molly would have sung, do re mi fa sol la ti, not me.

JIM: Molly, come back.

MOLLY: Not me. My feelings are hurt. Broken to pieces. (*She pushes the figurine in the shape of a woman off the counter. It crashes on the floor. Mack picks up the pieces.*)

JIM: Come back, Molly. (*Mack starts putting the pieces together.*)

MOLLY: Don't bother to put the pieces together, Mack. It will never be the same. Throw it away. (*Mack throws the pieces in a garbage can. The sound pains Molly.*) Goodbye, Molly . . . poor kid . . . she's gone. (*Taking the figure of Cupid.*) Perhaps you're too young to know how it hurts to love . . . It hurts. (*Molly and Jim stare at each other for a while. She looks away from him, showing her profile. She puts her foot up on the bar, puts a top hat on and her elbow on her knee.*) It seems I did my song after all. (*She rests her head on her hand.*)

MACK: OK, Molly, get off the bar.

MOLLY: Shut up, Mack.

JIM: Molly.

MACK: Get your feet off the bar. I won't have anybody putting their feet on the bar.

JIM: Leave her alone.

MACK: Who do you think you are? You come in here and look at the way she's acting. She's acting like a nut. She never acted like that before.

JIM: I know, I just broke her heart.

MACK: Molly.

MOLLY: Huh.

MACK: Look at her. (To Molly.) What's the matter with you?

MOLLY: Nothing is the matter with me. What are you talking about?

MACK: You're acting like a nut.

MOLLY: I'm not acting like a nut.

MACK: You better do something about her. I won't have anybody sitting at the bar.

JIM: I will. . . . (To Molly.) Molly.

MOLLY: What?

JIM: You used to be a nice kid.

MOLLY: No more. Those are bygone days.

MACK: Well, somebody bring the customer his drink, or I'm not responsible for my acts. (Molly takes a puff of her cigarette. Jim takes the drink to John as John goes to the bar.) What do you want?

JOHN: I thought I'd get the drink myself.

MACK: It's on the table. (John goes to his table.) I'm glad you brought him the drink, otherwise I couldn't have answered for my acts.

JIM: I didn't do it for you. I did it for her.

JOHN: Thanks, I was beginning to get thirsty.

JIM: That's all right. I did it for her. (Going to Molly.) Molly . . .

MOLLY: Hm.

JIM: Molly, I didn't mean to hurt you.

MOLLY: You can't hurt me. I have no heart.

JIM: You do, Molly, you have a heart.

MOLLY: I don't have a heart.

JIM: Molly, if I told you that I loved you, would you get off the bar?

MOLLY: No.

MACK: He's a sissy.

JIM: I am responsible . . . (He sings.)

I accept,
I accept,
I accept
The responsibility of my enormous sex appeal.
If a woman says she loves me,
I cannot tell her to go.

I breathe hot,
I breathe hot,

I breathe hot,
And I breathe hot.
No woman has ever resisted me, and I accept,
The responsibility.

J'accepte,
J'accepte,
J'accepte,
La responsabilité de mon énorme sex-appeal.
I cannot turn them away.
J'accepte
Les conséquences désastreuses de mon énorme sex-appeal.

I never said to a woman,
I love you.
But I accept
The responsibility.
HANGING WOMEN: (*Sing.*)
To a woman you will say,
I love you.
She will not understand.
You will say,
I love you.
You will say,
I love you, twice.
Twice you'll say it.
I love you. I love you.
And then she'll understand.
Je t'aime. Je t'aime.

(*Jim turns to Molly. His face is close to hers.*)

JIM: *Je t'aime.* (*Molly turns her head to look at Jim and does not reply.*) I love you.
(*Molly blows smoke in his face and smiles. Jim coughs. He is downcast. The Hanging Women move away from him. Jim walks to center stage and stands on his head with one leg bent and crossed, in a position resembling the Hanged Man of the Tarot.*)
HANGING WOMEN:
To a woman he said,
I love you.
She did not understand.
He said,
I love you.
But she did not understand.
He said,

I love you, twice.
Twice he said it.
Je t'aime. I love you.
And then she understood.
But not a word came out of her mouth.
Only smoke.
And he lost his charm.
All his charm was lost.

(*Spoken.*) Now, you're as common as Mack.

MACK: And who said I'm common, you dumb broads. I can take on the whole lot of you, you yellow-bellied broads. Bang, bang, bang, just like that.

(*Jim stands on his feet and sits at a table. The lights are dimmed except for a spot on Jim.*)

INTERLUDE

JIM: (*Sings.*)
And what has my noble face offered the world?
A smile.
Yes, it has done that.
A gentle look? Yes, my noble face has done that.
And what else have I offered the world?
A few kind words, perhaps.
And some elusive words.

And who am I?
Am I the wrongdoer or the wronged?

I never raised my hand to hurt a man.
And yet I ask: Who am I,
The wrongdoer or the wronged?

And what have my hands done?
They have reached out with love.
And the loved one has turned to me and said:
Who are you? . . . Who are you? . . .

I'm the wrongdoer.
That's who I am.

(*The lights come up.*)

PART II
Dracula the Misunderstood

(*There is no time lapse between Part One and Part Two.*)

JOHN: (*To Jim.*) Blackjack, sir?

JIM: What . . .

JOHN: Blackjack? (*Jim looks John over and nods. John shuffles the cards expecting Jim to come to his table. Jim pushes a chair away from his table with his foot inviting John to come to his. John shuffles the cards again, cuts them twice and looks at Jim. Jim challenges John by remaining where he is. John picks up the cards and holds them thinking what to do. Then, he puts two cards on the table face down and sneaks a look at Jim who remains seated. He looks at his card, then at Jim's and smiles feebly.*) You win. (*He goes to Jim. Through the following scene John puts a dollar on the table. Jim deals two cards each. One of the Hanging Women joins the players at their table and watches the game.*)

MOLLY: Give me a drink, Joe.

MACK: My name is not Joe.

MOLLY: Give me a drink.

MACK: What do you want?

MOLLY: Give me an absinthe.

MACK: You give me a pain. Did you guys hear that?

JOHN: What?

MACK: She wants an absinthe.

MOLLY: That's what we drink in the islands.

MACK: What islands? (*Molly thinks a while.*)

JIM: Make it two.

JOHN: Make it three.

MACK: (*Referring to Molly.*) Creep.

JOHN: Hit me. (*Jim gives John a card.*) Hit me again. (*Jim gives John a card.*) Hit me again. (*Jim gives John a card.*) Hit me again. (*Jim gives John a card.*) Hit me again.

JIM: How many cards have you got? You must be over.

JOHN: No, I'm not. Hit me again. (*Jim gives John a card suspiciously.*) Hit me again. (*They Indian-wrestle through the following scene. Mack puts three glasses on the counter.*)

MOLLY: Mack, set them up, Joe.

MACK: The name is Mack.

MOLLY: Set them up.

(*Molly walks to the players, and puts one foot up on the fourth chair. She puts a flower behind John's ear and kisses the Hanging Woman. Then, she considers a moment, takes the flower and puts it behind her own ear. Then she moves as if to kiss*)

John, changes her mind, puts the flower behind the Hanging Woman's ear. Then she takes the flower and holds it over her lips as she tries to remember such a scene from the film Morocco. *She then eats the flower. She starts walking toward the counter humming "One for My Baby." She is not satisfied with the song. Then starts humming "My Man." She is happier with that tune.*)

He isn't true.
He beats me too.
What can I do?

He isn't true.
He beats me too.
What can I do?

I don't really let anyone beat me.
MACK: So why do you keep saying it?
MOLLY: I like saying it.
MACK: *I like saying it. I like saying it.*
MOLLY: (*Sings.*)
He isn't true.
He beats me too.
What can I do?
MACK: Phony! You want a sock in the jaw? Why don't you guys do something about this dame? She gives me a pain. (*Molly takes a gun from the counter and puts a bullet through John's hand, which ends the Indian wrestling.*)
JIM: Thanks. (*To John.*) Stay?
JOHN: Hit me again. (*Jim gives John a suspicious and threatening look. John looks at the cards.*) I'm good.
JIM: (*Dealing himself a card.*) I'm busted.
JOHN: I win. (*John puts the two dollars on his side of the table.*)
JIM: Show me. (*John shuffles all cards and puts seven on the table. Jim puts the two dollars on his side of the table. They Indian-wrestle. Molly takes the gun and puts a bullet through Jim's hand.*)
JOHN: Thanks. (*John takes the two dollars, and puts one back on the table. He takes the cards.*) I'm dealer.
JIM: Forget it.
JOHN: What do you mean, forget it?
JIM: I'm not playing. (*To Mack.*) How about that drink? (*Mack signals Molly to take the drinks to the table. Molly throws the glasses over her shoulder, one at a time. Jim catches them and throws them back. They juggle the glasses for a while. Jim fails to catch them. They fall to his feet.*) You make me feel frustrated.
MOLLY: How's that?
JIM: First you hang on and you like it, and then you ignore me.
MOLLY: Who, me?
JIM: Yes, you.

(*Alberta enters. She wears a Shirley Temple wig and a child's dress*)

MACK: (*Signaling Molly to get Alberta out.*) Hey, Molly.

MOLLY: My name is not Molly.

JIM: What is your name?

MOLLY: I'm not telling anyone.

JIM: You could tell me.

MOLLY: I'm not telling.

JIM: What's the good of having a name if you don't tell anyone?

MOLLY: It's good. That way no one can call me.

JIM: I might want to write you a note.

MOLLY: I wouldn't read it anyway. (*She goes to John.*) Hey, handsome.

JIM: Don't talk to him. He's a fake.

MOLLY: What do you mean?

JIM: He never got laid in his life. (*John threatens Jim. The lights flash on and off.*)

ALBERTA: He's cute.

MACK: (*To Alberta.*) I told you, no children allowed. (*Alberta taps to a chair and sits. Mack taps her shoulder.*) Out. (*She ignores him. Mack takes her by the collar out the door.*) Yeah. You wouldn't believe it, would you? Smart aleck. Can't bear her. She dances all the time.

JOHN: She's an interesting-looking dame.

MOLLY: If you're not interested in me I was not interested in you first.

JIM: Can't even think straight.

MOLLY: I can think straight. I just don't want to.

JOHN: Let me have another drink. Don't give me anymore of that licorice stuff. Give me a man's drink.

MACK: Like what?

MOLLY: Absinthe is a man's drink. If you drink a lot of it you go blind.

JOHN: Give me an absinthe. (*He gives Jim an assertive look, then drinks the absinthe in one gulp.*) Yes, that child is certainly an interesting-looking dame. (*He gives Jim another assertive look and speaks to Mack.*) Let me have another one of those. I don't care if I go blind. (*Mack pours.*)

JIM: (*To himself.*) He never got laid in his life.

JOHN: I'll have another.

MACK: You didn't drink that one yet. (*He drinks it, belches several times and checks his vision.*)

JOHN: (*To Mack, attempting to be casual.*) Why do you think he said I never got laid?

MACK: Don't pay attention to him. He's a creep.

JOHN: Ask him.

MACK: Hey, why did you say . . .

JIM: All he's got is guns.

MACK: He's got more than guns. I bet you he's got more than guns.

JIM: (*Putting a dollar on the table.*) I bet all he's got is guns.

MACK: (*Putting a dollar on the table.*) I bet he's got more.

(*John does the "One Narrow Idea" dance. The dance consists of making the guns swing back and forth until he falls exhausted on the floor. The lights go to full intensity and remain so through the dance.*)

JOHN: (*Sings.*)
    One very long,
    Very narrow
    Idea.
    One very long
    And narrow
    Idea.

    A narrow idea.
    An old idea.
    A withered idea
    Without reward.
    A withering idea.
    An old, old idea.

MACK: (*Taking the two dollars.*) Yup, he's got more than guns.

JIM: (*Taking the two dollars from Mack.*) No, he doesn't. (*They Indian-wrestle. John helps Mack push Jim's arm down.*)

MACK: (*Taking the two dollars.*) Thanks.

JOHN: What did you think of that dance?

MACK: That was swinging, man.

JOHN: Was that swinging? Or wasn't that swinging?

MACK: That was swinging, man.

JOHN: Did you ever see anyone swing like that?

MACK: Not that I can remember.

JOHN: Try to remember. (*Mack thinks.*) Well? . . .

MACK: I can't remember.

JOHN: Try.

MACK: I said I can't remember.

JOHN: Then you never saw anyone swing like that.

MACK: I can't remember.

JOHN: If you can't remember it's because you never saw anyone swing like that.

MACK: I don't know.

JOHN: (*Twisting Mack's arm.*) What do you mean, you don't know?

MACK: I don't know.

JOHN: If you had, you would remember. (*Mack doesn't answer. John points his gun at Mack's temple.*) If you had, you would remember.

MACK: I suppose.

JOHN: Don't suppose. Did you or didn't you?

MACK: No, I never did.

JOHN: (*In narcissistic rapture.*) Ahhhhhhh.

MACK: Jesus! What a creep.

JOHN: Ask that lady in.

MACK: What lady?

JOHN: The one you turned out.

MACK: The child?

JOHN: Ask her in.

MACK: Jesus! (*Lights go back to normal. Mack goes to the door. On his way there he stops by Jim's table and gives him back his dollar.*)

MOLLY: (*To John.*) If that's your taste you don't belong in my book of names and telephones like a sailor. . . . I cross you out.

JOHN: What is she talking about?

MOLLY: If you like her.

MACK: Don't pay any attention to her.

JIM: Can't even speak English.

MOLLY: I can when I want to. . . . I only don't want to.

MACK: (*To Alberta.*) All right. You can come in. (*Alberta dances in. She sings and taps.*)

ALBERTA:

My two little feet,
Two little feet,
Tipity tap.
Tipity tap.
Tipity tap.

Tipity tap.
Tipity tap.
Tipity tap tap tap.

All the world says hi.
All the world says hi hi hi.

Dance to the harmony.
Dance to the rhythm.
Hotel bar butter.
I like to dance at cocktail time.
I like to dance at cocktail time.
I like to tap tap tap tap tap and dance.
Tap tap tap tap and dance.
Tap tap tap tap and dance.
I like to dance.

Dance to the harmony.
Dance to the rhythm.

Hotel bar butter.
Cocktails at cocktail time.
I like to dance at cocktail time.

Sing.
Sing it again.
Sh sh sh sh sh.
Sing it again.
Sh sh sh sh sh.
Sing it again.
I like to dance at cocktail time.

JIM: You know why you haven't grown?

JOHN: She's grown.

ALBERTA: Why?

JIM: Because you haven't been loved.

ALBERTA: Creep.

JIM: I thought you might want to know.

ALBERTA: No, I don't want to know. I am a child. That's why I haven't grown. And I get plenty of love, so leave me alone.

JIM: How old are you?

ALBERTA: Twenty-seven.

JIM: (*He considers a moment.*) You need love.

JOHN: This lady is with me if you don't mind.

JIM: No, I don't mind. But she should mind.

JOHN: Why should she mind?

ALBERTA: I don't mind. (*John presses Alberta's hand against his lips and remains in that position until he speaks again.*)

JIM: (*To Alberta.*) You need love. (*Alberta makes an obscene gesture to Jim.*)

MACK: (*Referring to Jim.*) Boy, he's finished.

JIM: What do you expect? You get involved with a broad like that and you're cooked. I didn't know she was German.

MOLLY: I was not German. I became German. You made me become German.

JIM: You always had it in you.

MOLLY: I am not a hen. I will not share my rooster with other hens. I'm the only hen or I'm not a hen.

JIM: She's crazy.

MOLLY: I may be crazy but I'm not a hen.

JIM: What's wrong with hens?

MOLLY: There's nothing wrong with hens. Only I'm not a hen.

JIM: I don't see why you had to be the only one. The others were happy.

MOLLY: But I'm not happy.

JIM: She's crazy.

MOLLY: I'm just wise and tough about you men.

JIM: I don't like tough women. I'm through with you.

MOLLY: I'm through with you before you are through with me.

JIM: Can't even speak English.

MOLLY: Only when I get angry. (*She goes to the bird cage and sets the bird free.*) Fly away mine *kleiner Vogel*, baby. *Esse alle Würmer die du kannst.* That means: fly away my little bird. Eat all the worms you can. Fly away mine *kleiner Vogel*, baby. *Esse alle Würmer die du kannst.* (*The Hanging Women surround Molly.*) No . . . no . . . no . . . (*The Hanging Women giggle and go back to their places.*)

JIM: Creep.

MOLLY: Little man. (*Jim goes to John and Alberta.*)

MACK: His pride is hurt.

JIM: No, it is not. I just think there's something wrong with her. (*To John and Alberta.*) May I join you?

JOHN: If the lady wishes.

ALBERTA: All right. But don't tell me I'm a hen.

JIM: I never told you you were a hen.

ALBERTA: I mean, OK, but don't tell me I need love.

JIM: OK. (*He sits.*)

JOHN: Madam? . . .

ALBERTA: Sir? . . .

JOHN: Would you like anything to drink?

ALBERTA: I'll have a mint julep with cherry syrup.

JOHN: (*To Jim.*) Would your lady friend like a drink?

JIM: I have no lady friend. Can't you see I have no lady friend? (*He gives Molly a dirty look.*)

ALBERTA: You don't have to get rude. You have no lady friend because you have no manners.

JOHN: (*To the Hanging Woman.*) Would you like a drink, madam? (*The Hanging Woman smiles.*)

JIM: Why aren't you with the others? (*The Hanging Woman joins the others.*) Creep!

JOHN: (*To Mack.*) A mint julep with cherry syrup. . . . Make it two.

JIM: See? He's not real. He just drinks what everybody else drinks.

ALBERTA: I still like him better than you. Even if he's not real.

JOHN: I'm real. Can't you see I'm real? (*He pinches himself and shakes the table.*) Could I have done that if I weren't real?

ALBERTA: You're real. It's he who is not real. (*John presses Alberta's hand against his lips.*)

JIM: (*Dismissing the subject.*) I'm real.

ALBERTA: (*Referring to John.*) And besides being real, he's cute.

JOHN: My peach. (*He presses her hand against his lips again.*)

JIM: You see what I mean? He's not real.

ALBERTA: He looks real to me.

JOHN: My peach . . . my pearl . . . (*He presses Alberta's hand against his lips.*)

JIM: He's just pretending to be real. That's why he kisses you.

ALBERTA: (*Hitting Jim on the head*) He's not pretending. He kisses me because he likes my baby flesh . . . and you stop bothering us. We want to be alone. Sit somewhere else.

JOHN: My peach, my pearl, my persimmon, I want to be alone with you. My peach, my pearl, when the impossible begins to seem possible. When love knocks at our door. All our expectations, dreams, desires go rampant. There is no end to what seems possible. There is no end to what we ask for. Sugar baby, candy child, give me your life.

ALBERTA: (*Matter-of-fact.*) No. (*John picks Alberta up. He looks for a place to take her. He is like a wild beast looking for a place to take his prey. She gets away from him. He runs after her.*)

HANGING WOMEN: (*Sing.*)
Is this true passion,
Or the way a vain man has
Of saying to himself:
I am not dead?

JOHN:
I am not dead.
Not dead.
Not dead.

HANGING WOMEN:
Is this true love?
True love?
True love?

One very long,
Very narrow,
Very old idea.
An old idea.
A long idea.
An old, old,
Withered idea,
Without reward.

A withering idea.
One very narrow,
Very old idea.
A narrow idea.

ALBERTA: Me, the little darling. The heaven on earth. The night without pain The honey of the flowers. I will not be yours. Ever. . . . I can't. . . . I'm pure.

JOHN: My fairy tale, my peach, my pearl, grant me my wish.

ALBERTA: No.

JOHN: I am in control of my emotions. I always have been. Once I was almost in love. Yes, indeed, no one can say I've never loved. I am an important man.

My scope is very narrow. Yes, it's very narrow, but it is wide enough to strike a pose of self-importance. . . . That's all I need. . . . Me, a failure? Never! I'm in control of my emotions. My emotions are feeble. Me, strong. The more I'm known to strangers the more I lose my sense of dignity. I have no point of view. I am well known, that's all I need. You know me. I know myself. What, me, get old? Never! That's not for me. Candy child, give me your life.

ALBERTA: No.

(*John moves behind Alberta and sinks his teeth into her neck. Through the following song John and Alberta take vampirical love-making poses. Between the poses, and with the aid of the Hanging Women, they do a costume change with rapid choreographed movements. John removes his guns and his hat and puts on a cape. Alberta takes her wig off, letting her hair loose. Her dress grows long to the floor. He looks like a vampire. She is sensuous and glamorous. He sinks his teeth into her neck again.*)

HANGING WOMEN: (*Sing.*)
    Is this true passion,
    Or the way a vain man has
    Of saying to himself:
    I am not dead?

    Is this true love?
    True love?
    True love?

(*John lifts his head and looks around. He moves in front of Alberta and stretches his arms as if to protect her.*)

JOHN: Don't anyone touch my own. She's mine.

JIM: Who wants to.

JOHN: My one and only. My own.

MACK: Creep.

JOHN: Ahhh. Love, love, love. . . . (*He does a pirouette.*) I feel at last alive. (*He dances around with movements resembling a lizard's. He then takes Alberta to the mirror. By means of rear projection one sees Alberta in the mirror but not John. He moves away from her in terror and shame. To Alberta, from a distance.*) Tell me that you see me. (*She takes a step back.*) Tell me that you love me. (*She looks away from him.*) Kiss me. Ahhh. My love recoils from me. (*He sits down at a table. He is downcast. Alberta takes two steps toward him but stops. He watches her.*)
My lady said the hair around my temple
Is different from the rest,
And that it is a sight to behold.

She said it is smooth and grows downward,
While the rest grows wild.

My lady said there's a line
From the back of my ear to my shoulder
That gives her pleasure to look at.
And she said as a present
She'll give me a flock of birds.
She is my love.
That lady is my love.

She speaks of love
Only angels know,
And yet she fears me.
My lady fears me.

(*She moves toward him.*)

My lady said
The joint that holds my jaw to my skull
Is delicate like a bird's.
So my lady said.

My lady said my face is life itself.
She is my love.
That lady is my love,
And yet, she fears me.

My lady said when she held me in her arms
She held not a man but the world.
And yet my lady fears me.
She fears me.

(*Alberta goes to John. She brings her hand to his cheek and kisses him.*)

ALBERTA: (*Sings.*)
    The senses are five:
    Sight, smell, hearing, taste, touch.
    Los sentidos. Les sens. I sentiti.
    The verb to sense in French
    Refers to smelling, "*sens.*"
    Tu sens bon.
    In Italian, "*sentire,*"
    It refers to hearing.
    Sente amore mio.
    In Spanish, "*sentir,*"
    Means to feel.

Siento en la alma
Unas ganas intensas de llorar.
In English to sense
Is nothing you can put your finger on.
I sense something unusual all around me.

Love, love, love. Love, love, love, love.
You have brought me to my senses
You have made sense of me
And the sense of me is you.
I hear. I see. I smell. I taste. I touch.
Oh, love.
My life is senseless without you.

(*They kiss. His back is to the audience. A cape he wears rolled up around his neck is let down. The cape bears an "S." John is now Superman. He turns around. An "S" is visible on his chest. They circle around the stage as if strolling in the park. The Hanging Women surround them singing. When they reach the center of the stage they each circle the stage in opposite directions. Half the Hanging Women follow John, the other half follow Alberta. They meet in the center again, and walk down the aisle, followed by the Hanging Women who carry garlands.*)

HANGING WOMEN: (*Sing.*)
    She is my love.
    That lady is my love.
    She speaks of love
    Only angels know.
MACK: Molly, that kid is doing better than you.
MOLLY: No, she is not.
MACK: Yes she is.
HANGING WOMEN:
    She is my love.
    That lady is my love.
    She speaks of love
    Only angels know. (*They exit.*)
JIM: Fiddlesticks. (*There is a short pause and a sense of sadness.*) Yeah, that's how
    it is.
MOLLY: Mack, play something amusing, Sam. I feel sad. (*They are silent for a
    moment. Molly sighs.*)
JIM: I beg your pardon?
MOLLY: Hm.
JIM: A second chance?
MOLLY: Hm.
JIM: Hm, hm. Not me. I'm quitting. . . . You had your chance. (*They recite the*

following.)
MOLLY:
　To tell you I still love you?
　Why? You care?
　I loved you once.
　What? You think that's nothing?
　It isn't everyone who's loved the way I loved you.
　You're feeling sorry now.
　Well, too late, I'm quitting.
　You can't expect me to survive all that.
JIM:
　I'm too proud. You're right.
　And you're a two-time loser.
　Once you had my love and didn't take it.
　That makes it once you were the loser.
　And now you want me back.
　You lose again.
　I'm too proud, you're right.
　I'm quitting.
　I'm not expected to survive all that.

(*Jim walks to the door. He and Molly start singing with their backs to each other.*)

JIM & MOLLY:
　A sense of incompletion . . . yeah . . . yeah . . .
　A joke without a laugh,
　A friend who doesn't hear,
　A promise without hope,
　An offer withdrawn,
　A goodbye with no departure.
　And what? Am I expected to survive all that?
　Ha ha. Fat chance. Not me. I'm quitting.
JIM:
　Johnny told me, August first,
　There'll be a parade.
　Ha ha. If the city permits.
MOLLY:
　Ronnie told me, August second,
　We'll see a movie.
　Ha ha. He changed his mind.
JIM:
　My horoscope said, August third,
　I'd have good news.

Ha ha. There was no news.

MOLLY:

Mack told me, August fourth,
He'd give me a raise.
Ha ha. There was no raise.

JIM:

My cousin told me, August fifth,
We'd go for a ride.
Ha ha. The car broke down.

MOLLY:

August sixth, I took the bus.
It was a long ride,
And when I got there,
No one said hello.

JIM & MOLLY:

And what? Am I expected to survive all that?
Ha, ha. That's all I can say.
Ha ha. Ha ha. Ha ha.

(*Jim walks to the door. He turns back and shakes hands with Molly.*)

JIM: Goodbye.

MOLLY: Goodbye. (*He walks to the door again.*) You know . . .

JIM: . . . What? . . .

MOLLY: In order to become what we are . . .

JIM: Yes? . . .

MOLLY: We have to go through many stages.

JIM: Yes.(*Molly puts on the top hat. They laugh.*)

MOLLY: If we had met some other time . . . perhaps . . .

JIM: Perhaps we'll meet again some other time.

MOLLY: Yes.

JIM: I'll be going now. (*He walks to the door.*) See you later . . . Molly?

MOLLY: (*Taking the hat off.*) Yes . . .

JIM: You'll wait for me?

MOLLY: I will. . . . Will you recognize me?

JIM: Yes, I'll know you.

(*They wave. He exits. Molly walks to the table where she first fell asleep. She leans her head on the table. Mack walks in and straightens the place, leaving it as in the beginning of the play. The Young Man enters. He carries luggage which resembles in color the Hanging Women's costumes. He looks at Molly.*)

MACK: She's lost to the world. What would you have?

YOUNG MAN: Do you rent rooms?

MACK: No, we don't rent rooms.

YOUNG MAN: (*Picking up the luggage.*) Oh, well . . . (*The lights flash on and off. The Young Man puts the luggage down and turns to look at Molly.*) On second thought, I think I'll have a drink.

MACK: What would you like?

YOUNG MAN: Double rye. (*Mack pours the drink. The Young Man pays Mack and takes the drink to a table.*) I'll give my feet a rest. I walked from the station.

(*Mack exits. The Young Man watches Molly. He drinks his drink, takes a deep breath, picks up his bags, and exits. The lights fade except for a blue spot on Molly's head. She wakes up suddenly and looks where the Young Man sat. The spot is held for a few seconds while two high musical notes play. The spot fades.*)

END

A Vietnamese Wedding

A *Vietnamese Wedding* was first enacted at Washington Square Methodist Church in New York on February 4, 1967, as part of the week-long cumulative protest against American involvement in Vietnam called Angry Arts Week. The following participated as readers:

Remy Charlip, Maria Irene Fornes, Aileen Passloff, Florence Tarlow.

118

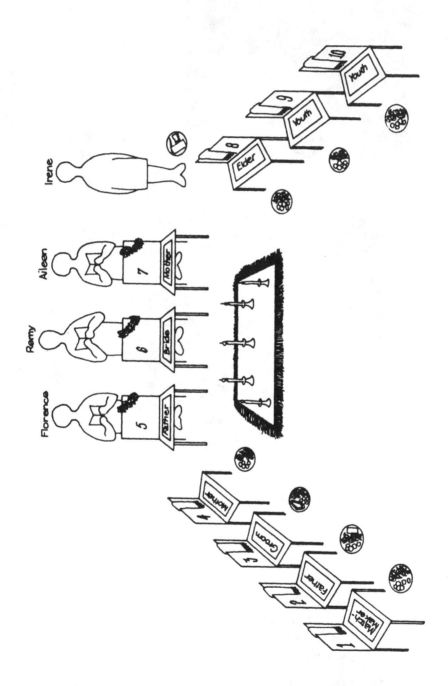

The following objects are to be set in the manner indicated in the diagram:

10 Chairs
10 5x7 Cards
 3 Flower garlands (about 24" around)
 7 Red sashes (about 5' long)
 8 Red trays or plates
   Areca leaves (or a substitute)
   Betel nuts (or a substitute)
 1 Ring
 1 Necklace
 1 Bracelet
 3 Bags of chocolate money
 2 3x5 Cards
 1 Colorful floor mat
 5 Candles and holders
 1 Sheet of red rice paper
 1 Match box
 1 Pen
 4 Whistles
 4 Noisemakers
 1 Tape of Vietnamese music (*Music of Vietnam*, Ethnic Folkways Library FE
   4352, is suggested)

The ten 5x7 cards will indicate the position of the participants and will be placed on the chairs as shown in the diagram. The flower wreaths are to be placed on the back of chairs 5, 6, 7. The read sashes are to be placed on the back of chairs 1, 2, 3, 4, 8, 9, 10. Seven trays are to be placed on the floor facing chairs 1, 2, 3, 4, 8, 9, 10. They are to contain areca leaves and betel nuts. Besides these, the Groom's tray will contain the ring, the necklace, and the bracelet; the Father of the Groom's will contain the 3 chocolate money bags and a 3x5 card with the following speech:

Friends, neighbors, and
newly acquired family; may we take
your daughter to our house?

The second 3x5 card should have the following speech:

Friends, neighbors, and
newly acquired family; we allow you
to take our daughter to your house.

and should be held by Florence.

The eighth red tray should be in a place accessible to Irene, and will contain the pen, the matches and the red rice paper with the following message:

Rose Silk Thread God,
look after our marriage.

Florence, Remy, Aileen, and Irene will hold the whistles and noisemakers and use them at the end of the piece.

A *Vietnamese Wedding* is not a play. Rehearsals should serve the sole purpose of getting the readers acquainted with the text and the actions of the piece. The four people conducting the piece are hosts to the members of the audience who will enact the wedding, and their behavior should be casual, gracious, and unobtrusive.

(*Florence, Remy, Aileen, and Irene stand as indicated in the diagram.*)

REMY: We are going to present to you a Vietnamese wedding. And we are going to ask a few of you to help us. What you have to do is very simple. It doesn't require any acting ability, and we will tell you what to do as we go along. First, we'll choose the matchmaker.

(*Remy chooses the members of the wedding party from the audience. Irene, Florence, and Aileen help them to their seats, and help them put on their sashes around their waists and garlands on their heads.*)

Then, we'll choose the father and the mother of the bride.
Then, the father and the mother of the groom.
Then, the groom.
Then, we choose the bride.
Now, the distinguished elder member of the groom's family.
And then, two young members of the groom's family.

(*Florence, Remy, Aileen, and Irene return to their positions.*)

FLORENCE: In Vietnam, especially in the cities, there are young people who have rebelled against traditional customs. That is, they prefer to take it upon themselves to choose their own marital partner as they do in western countries. However, for the most part, Vietnamese youths follow tradition. Marriages are arranged by the parents with the aid of an experienced matchmaker. The matching of a pair is a complex and delicate matter. It requires the love and wisdom of parents, plus the objective judgment of a matchmaker. The bride and groom must be of equal social standing, equal education, and their moral history must also be equal. Once the bride and groom are chosen according to these standards, their horoscopes are drawn. If the horoscopes indicate that their characters are not compatible or that there might be conflict between them at some point in their lives, another mate is chosen.

AILEEN: If a family is asked for their daughter or son in marriage, and they wish to refuse the offer without offending the suitor's family, they speak to the astrologer privately.

FLORENCE: If the offer is acceptable and the charts propitious, the wedding date is chosen.

REMY: (*To the Bride.*) When is your birthday? (*The Bride answers. To provide an example we will say she has answered May fifth. Remy then passes the information on to Florence.*) May fifth.

(*Florence looks up the date in the accompanying chart and replies.*)

January 1-20: Capricorn
January 21-31: Aquarius
February 1-19: Aquarius
February 20-28: Pisces
March 1-20: Pisces
March 21-31: Aries
April 1-19: Aries
April 20-30: Taurus
May 1-20: Taurus
May 21-31: Gemini
June 1-21: Gemini
June 22-30: Cancer
July 1-21: Cancer
July 22-31: Leo
August 1-21: Leo
August 22-31: Virgo
September 1-22: Virgo
September 23-30: Libra
October 1-22: Libra
October 23-31: Scorpio
November 1-21: Scorpio
November 22-30: Sagittarius
December 1-21: Sagittarius
December 22-31: Capricorn

FLORENCE: Taurus.

REMY: (*To the Groom.*) When is your birthday?

(*The Groom answers. We will say he was born November fifth.*)

REMY: (*To Florence.*) November fifth.

(Florence looks up the date in the chart.)

FLORENCE: Scorpio

REMY: Taurus and Scorpio. Very good!

AILEEN: Very, very good!

FLORENCE: Excellent!

REMY: Formerly, girls were wed as young as thirteen and boys at sixteen. The reason for early marriages was usually economic. For some families, to give their daughter away meant one less mouth to feed. For others, to gain a daughter meant one more person to help with the housework. For some, the addition of a male meant another helping hand in the field. There was no general rule as to whether it was convenient to add or to subtract one number in the family. It depended on the particular needs of each household. These early marriages were usually satisfactory to the family, but as the young people grew, it happened occasionally that they did not find their mate to their liking. A young woman tells us about her unhappy marriage in this popular poem:

AILEEN:
My mother was greedy.
She wanted
A basket of rice,
A fat pig,
And a Hang Kung tail.

I asked her to refuse.
But she said I was
Too young to know,
And brought me to my groom.

Now I am fully grown.
I am tall and my husband is short.

We are like a pair of unequal chopsticks.

REMY: Child marriages are no longer common in Vietnam.

AILEEN: Though many things have changed, the wedding ritual remains the same. The betel nut and the areca leaf are symbolic of love and good will, and they are always exchanged as a most valuable offering between the bride's and the groom's families. The custom derives from an ancient myth.

FLORENCE: During the reign of Hung Wung III, there was a mandarin named Cao, who had two beautiful sons, Tan and Sung. One day, the mandarin and his wife died, and the two boys were left without a father, a mother, a house, or money. The boys had to go from town to town looking for work, and they could find none.

One day they came to the house of Magistrate Luu who happened to be a friend of their father Cao. Luu received the boys in his house, and said: "I never had a son and now I have two." It was true that Magistrate Luu didn't have a son, but he had a daughter who was as fair as a white lotus and as fresh as a spring rose. Naturally, both boys loved her the moment they saw her. But neither of them spoke to her of his love because each knew his brother also loved her.

Luu realized what was happening. He knew that the boys would become old and shriveled before they spoke to the maiden. To prevent that from happening, he decided he would follow the custom and give his daughter to the eldest. One day he said to Sung: "Which one of you is the eldest?" And Sung said: "Tan is the eldest," but Tan quickly said: "Sung is the eldest." Only one of them was telling the truth. But Luu, who was a very clever fellow, decided he would not ask any more questions. He knew the boys would keep giving him the same answers. Instead, that night for dinner, he placed only one pair of chopsticks between the brothers.

When dinner was served, Sung, without giving it any thought, picked up the chopsticks and handed them to Tan. And Tan, without giving it any thought, received the chopsticks and bent down to eat, as any older brother would. "I found you out," said Luu to Tan. "You are the eldest. You will marry my daughter."

REMY: Tan was now the happiest of men in all of Vietnam. He spent all his time taking walks with his new bride, reciting poetry to her, and singing love songs.

Sung overcame his love for the fair maiden and accepted his lot, for he wanted only joy and happiness for his beloved brother. But after a while, he realized that he was very lonely. He sat alone in his room waiting for a sign of care, or friendship, from Tan . . . but nothing happened.

In wild sorrow, he ran away from home, for he could stand the sadness no more. He ran and ran, passing leafy forests and flat meadows, until he reached the dark blue sea. Night came and Sung fell exhausted onto the ground, hungry and thirsty. His head was as hot as fire. And he cried and cried until he died and was turned into a white chalky rock.

When Tan realized his brother was gone, he went after him. He passed leafy forests and the flat meadows and he arrived at the same dark blue sea. He too was exhausted. He sat down by the white chalky rock, and he cried and cried until he died. And he was turned into a tree with a straight stem and green palms. It was the areca tree.

AILEEN: The lovely maiden missed her husband so much that she set off one day to look for him. She went along the same way as the brothers and reached the sea and lay down exhausted at the foot of the tall areca tree. Tears of despair rolled down her cheeks and she cried sorrowfully until she died. She was turned into a creeping plant—the betel—which twined around the lofty trunk of the areca tree.

That night, all the people in the village nearby had the same dream. They all dreamt the story of Tan, Sung and the maiden. The strange occurrence came to the ears of King Hung Wung III, who said: "If they were so devoted to each other, let us mix the three things, the rock, the areca leaf, and the betel nut, and see what happens." They burned the rock, which became white and soft, and they wrapped it in an areca leaf. Then they cut a piece of betel nut, and squeezed them all together. The mixture became liquid and red, like blood. The king then said: "This is the true symbol of conjugal and fraternal love. Let the tree and the plant be grown everywhere to remind us of true devotion and love. And let us chew the betel nut so that affection and good will will reign among us."

FLORENCE: The habitual chewing of the betel nut produces a blackening effect on the teeth, until they appear as though they have been lacquered. In the past, such black teeth were an object of admiration. A young man tells us about his loved one's teeth in a popular poem:

REMY:
Do you remember me when you go home?
When I go home I remember your teeth.

I would pay one hundred taels
For your beautiful lips.

But for your black teeth
I would pay much more.

AILEEN: The wedding ceremony.

FLORENCE: The procedure is very formal. The date and hour must be exact, according to horoscopic readings. Everybody wears his best clothing. The boy's family wears red sashes around their waists.

REMY: The boy's family walks from the boy's home to the girl's home in a ceremonial procession.

(Irene tells the members of the Groom's party to stand and pick up their trays. She leads them in a procession around the theatre aisles, while Aileen reads the following speech. The Vietnamese music is played softly.)

AILEEN: The matchmaker has previously discussed the amount and kind of gifts. As the gifts are to be distributed among the bride's family and friends, the larger the family the more gifts are required. If the groom's family is rich, the gifts will include sacks of grain, live animals, clothing, candles, incense, tea, cakes, betel nuts and areca leaves, but no matter how poor the family is, there will always be betel nuts and areca leaves.

FLORENCE: The gifts are placed on the ancestral altar by the groom's party.

(Irene instructs the party to place the trays on the altar [floor mat]. Then she instructs the Groom and his Father to stand to the left of the altar, and the rest to the right.)

REMY: The candles are lit.

(*Irene lights the candles with the help of some of the Groom's family. The music stops.*)

AILEEN: The bridegroom gives the bride jewels—an engagement ring, a necklace and a bracelet.

(*If the Groom doesn't act of his own accord, Irene will tell him what to do. The same applies to any of the following directions.*)

FLORENCE: The father of the groom gives the bride, her father, and her mother a certain amount of money. (*He does.*)

REMY: The groom's father makes a solemn request to take the bride away to their home. (*The Groom's Father reads the card on his plate.*) Solemnly the father of the bride agrees. (*Florence gives the Father of the Bride his card to read. He reads it out loud.*) Then they all bow three times. (*Everyone bows three times. Irene stands next to the Groom with her tray.*)

AILEEN: A message to the genie of marriage, the Rose Silk Thread God, is written on a red sheet of paper. (*Irene gives the red paper to the Groom to sign.*) Then, it is burned, so that the message will reach the genie. (*The Groom burns the message.*)

FLORENCE: At this point, the couple is considered married. (*Irene tells the Groom to take the Bride by the hand and head the procession.*) And a party is held with a lot of speechmaking, gift-giving, and merrymaking. (*Irene leads the procession, going first around the readers, then, along the aisles. The music starts softly while Remy reads.*) The groom's family traditionally acts as though they are very anxious to take the bride to their home. The groom's entourage then begins the trip home in the form of a procession with the bride and her attendants, friends, and relatives joining in. Little children sometimes set up roadblocks and ask tolls of the wedding party. These are readily paid, as they consider it bad luck to refuse.

FLORENCE: Upon arrival at the groom's house, the party is met by the loud noise of firecrackers.

(*The music plays loudly. Florence, Remy, and Aileen join the procession, and blow their whistles. Irene also blows her whistle and leads the procession out of the theatre.*)

END

Dr. Kheal

Dr. Kheal was first performed on April 15, 1968, in two simultaneous productions: one at the Village Gate, as a benefit for the Caffe Cino, and one at the New Dramatists Workshop. Both versions were directed by Remy Charlip. At the Village Gate the performer was David Tice; at the New Dramatists Workshop it was Phillip Bruns.

(There is a reading stand, a small table with a jug of water and two glasses, a blackboard, and a stand with various charts, and a pointer. Professor Kheal enters. He is small, or else the furniture is large.)

DR. KHEAL: The Professor picks up the chalk, (*Dr. Kheal picks up the chalk*) and writes. (*Dr. Kheal writes The Outline on the blackboard. He looks at what he wrote and draws a line along the edges of the blackboard. As he is drawing the line he becomes distracted and the motion of the chalk becomes slower.*) He looks at the class with an air of superiority and counts to three demanding their attention. One, two and three. He asks his first question. (*He mouths a question and then puts his hand to his ear as if listening to the answer.*) Wrong. (*Pointing in different directions.*) Wrong. Wrong. Wrong. Wrong. Then, suddenly, someone shouts his answer from the back. Others join him. They all shout at once. It becomes a loud and fast thing. The teacher speaks rapidly, trying to reply to each. Wrong, wrong, wrong, wrong, wrong, wrong, wrong. Damn it! You're wrong. (*Suggesting a voice from the distance.*) "Dear Professor, perhaps you have the wrong answer." (*He looks at the audience fiercely.*) My answer wrong? It couldn't be that my answer is wrong. I am the master. Let us proceed. (*He looks among his papers, then talks to himself.*) How could my answer be wrong? . . . Hmmm . . . Did I have an answer? (*He thinks.*) Nonsense, I don't need an answer. I am the master . . . Let me see . . . Let me see . . . I'll find an answer. Hmmm . . . Hmmm . . . How is that possible? I don't even remember the question. Was there a question? (*To the audience.*) Was there? (*To himself.*) Hmm. Of course there was. There's always a question, and who knows what the answer is? (*To the audience.*) Raise your hand if you know the answer. . . . Ha ha. There you are! There are many of you, but the multitude is often wrong. (*He starts to erase the blackboard.*) Is it not?

(*He looks to see if someone replies. He erases the blackboard and writes* On Poetry.) Now, poetry is for the most part a waste of time, and so is politics . . . and history . . . and philosophy. . . . Nothing concrete. Nothing like a well-made box. Which is concrete and beautiful and you can put things in it. But what can you do with poems? Tell me. And with politics, and with history, and with philosophy?—You can wrap them up, shove them up your ass, and what do you have? (*He moves his hands as if he were doing a magic trick which ends with the middle finger up.*) . . . Nothing . . . Ha ha ha ha ha ha. (*Invaded by an immense poetic feeling.*) But if you can make a box, think, have you not made a lyrical thing? (*He thinks he hears someone speak. He squints, and looks over his glasses, then ignores the possible speaker.*) Poetry, on the other hand, is just a few words put together. Just a few. Just words. There is poetry . . . And then they say there are poets . . . poets of this sort, poets of that sort, and poets of the other sort . . . But who, tell me, understands the poetry of space in a box? I do . . . Abysmal and concrete at the same time. Four walls, a top, and a bottom . . . and yet a void. . . . Who understands that? I, Professor Kheal, I understand it clearly and expound it well! (*He takes a deep breath.*) And then, there is the smell of wood, that sober smell.

(*He goes to the blackboard and writes* On Balance. *Then, he draws the following figure.*)

(*He moves away, looks at the blackboard, looks for his glasses in his pocket, puts them on, and points to the blackboard.*) Balance can save your life. Imbalance can destroy it. (*Lost in his thoughts.*) . . . What is balance? . . . Balance is a state of equilibrium between opposing forces. The harmonious proportions of elements in design. Balance is keeping my pants up. My groin in place. (*He looks around with raised eyebrows for a moment.*) Any more questions?

(*He goes to the blackboard, erases, and writes* On Ambition.) Then, of course there is the question of will. Will, will, will, will. Always will. Tell me, does anyone here know the answer. (*He waits for an answer.*) Does anyone know the nature of will? (*He waits for an answer.*) Does the thing happen, or does one do it? . . . Through will. Does the thing happen, or does one do it? Of course, sometimes it happens and other times one does it. I don't mean . . . just anything . . . ordinarily . . . I mean how . . . what . . . which . . . Is it made? . . . Can *it* be made? . . . What? Life! Of course, life. No, I don't mean birth. I mean life. Can I make my own life . . . Of course not, you fool. A well-planned life is pitiful. Doesn't it seem richer if the firmament puts its silvery hands in it? In your life? (*He puts his hand to his ear.*) What? (*He listens.*) Not modern? . . . Mo-dern? . . . (*He scrutinizes the speaker.*) You scum, you turd, you stale refuse. Worse than that! Plastic face! (*He blows air through his mouth.*) That is what I think of you. . . . I'll take your will and chew on it, like a little oyster, or a clam. Chew, chew, chew, your little will, yum, yum . . . Can you make a clam? I'll chew your little entrails. (*He darts his tongue like a satyr. Then he puts his hands over his groin with a scared look. He looks around the audience.*) Can you make a clam? I don't mean stuffed clam. I mean—make—a—clam. What would you like? A show of hands? All right. Let's have a show of hands. Those in favor of the firmament leading you by the hand, raise your hands. (*He counts.*) Those in favor of making your own life raise your hands. (*He counts.*) All I can do is peepee before you. (*He raises his leg like a dog and then shakes it.*) And the rest, those who didn't raise your hands—what do you think? Is there another alternative? Either you do it or else it does itself. Life, that is. What other way is there? None. (*He looks suspiciously at a few.*) None. There is no other way. All right.

(*He erases the blackboard and writes* On Energy. *He goes to the chart stand and takes the pointer.*) Here is the next question. (*He unrolls a chart that reads: How does one do a million little things?*) How does one do a million little things? . . . What is the answer? (*Pointing.*) How—does—one—do—a—million—lit-tle—things? (*He waits a moment for the answer. He speaks with excitement.*) One at a time! (*He is pleased with the incisiveness of his answer.*) Now. (*He unrolls the next chart. It reads: How does one do a million big things?*) How—does —one—do—a—million—big—things? . . . Hmmm . . . Does anyone know the answer? (*He waits a moment.*) One at a time. Ha ha ha ha ha . . . What a surprise . . . Surprised, everyone? Now, the last of three. (*He unrolls the next chart. It reads: How does one do one big thing?*) How—does—one—do—one—big—thing? . . . Ha ha ha ha ha ha ha . Extraordinary question, isn't it? I'll answer it. (*He goes to the blackboard and makes this drawing.*)

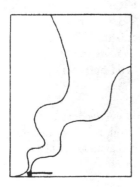

(*Pointing to where the arrow indicates.*) Start here. (*He fills in the space as follows and continues upward with very rapid moves.*)

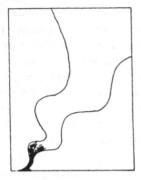

(*He darts his tongue like a satyr.*) Would you have guessed? Never.

(*He erases the blackboard and writes* On Truth.) Now . . . words change the nature of things. A thing not named and the same thing named are two different things. Ha ha ha ha . . . The ways of the Devil . . . that son of a gun . . . Someone once said, "In the beginning was the word." Guess who? The Devil . . . clever bastard. He'd say anything. In our time he's still renaming things. Freedom! Ah . . . You see? I'm right, Happiness! Today who dares to say the word without some kind of (*mocking their manner*) "Intellectual hesitation." (*Still mockingly.*) "Happiness . . . happiness . . . What is happiness?" (*Back to himself.*) And I show them my teeth. (*He opens his mouth wide, then puts his fingers in his mouth.*) And I say to them, there is happiness. My teeth are good. (*Forcing his hand in the mouth of an imaginary person.*) And I put my whole hand in their mouths and I call them every name in the book. Violent! I am. I get angry. But it doesn't matter. I am always right. You see, people believe that truth is the order in which they live. Others, the bright ones, believe that there is no truth at all but only an arrangement. Both are mistaken. Ha ha ha ha ha ha. Now, truth is not at all the way we understand things to be. Why? The moment you name it, it is gone. A chair. You name it: "Chair," and there it is, still a chair. A dog. You name it: "Dog," and it comes. But truth . . . you name it and it vanishes. What is truth then? Anyone know? (*He stands like a bullfighter and makes three rapid passes.*) There is truth. Three quick passes. Name it here, here, and here. Surround it, and you'll have it. Never touch it. It will vanish.

(*He goes to the blackboard and erases. Then he writes* Anecdote.) On my way here this evening someone said to me . . . "Dr. Kheal, is being poor a sign of stinginess?" (*He opens his mouth as if to laugh, but makes no sound.*) I said, no, it isn't. (*Pause.*) But of course it is. (*Pause.*) Ha ha ha ha.

(*He erases the blackboard and writes* On Beauty and Love.) The morning was fine. I cleaned the bathroom, then the kitchen. What else is there but cleanliness? (*He looks over his glasses expecting objections.*) And then, I lay down to rest with my head on a high pillow. "Gee, look at my belly going up and down. I must be alive." Well . . . in that case . . . I go to my dresser, I look in the mirror. "Gee, look how pleasant my face is in the mirror, I must be beautiful." Ha ha ha. Well, we each have our way. I know that we can only do what is possible. I know that. We can only do what is possible for us to do. But still it is good to know what the impossible is. (*There is a pause. He is looking at the impossible.*) Beauty is . . . the impossible . . . Beauty . . . beauty . . . beauty . . . what art thou that drives me out of my mind? Beauty . . . Shall I tell you?

(*He sees Crissanda in front of him.*) She speaks in riddles, like the gods. "ksjdnhyidfgesles." She says: (*He chants the following in a feminine voice.*) "I am the supreme lover. I bring you bliss. . . . Listen to me . . . Listen . . . I know . . ." (*In his own voice.*) The fool, she knows nothing. (*Lovingly.*) It's the way she talks, in riddles, like the gods. "ksjdudyehrs." She says: (*Chanting again.*) "Don't move your hands when you talk. It tickles me. From the distance, the movements of your hands tickle me." (*Back to himself.*) And I laugh. . . . And I move my hands. Ha ha ha ha. (*He pauses. He looks at Crissanda.*) And she looked at me surprised, and her little eye wanders and is lost. (*He watches her vanish.*) "Where are you?" I said, "My little one . . . Crissanda . . . don't go . . . I didn't mean to laugh." And she said: "Crazy people are fools. (*Making his voice faint.*) You fool . . . you fool . . . you fool . . ." (*His eyes are open very wide. They are filled with tears.*) And she left. "Crissanda, Crissanda," I called after her . . . She was gone. . . . What happened? What happened . . . I know what happened and yet I cannot say. I do not know the words to speak of beauty and love. I, who know everything . . . Some things are impossible. . . .

(*He goes back to the blackboard.*) Love, as we know it, increases daily. Let us say the average level of love is 100 degrees. We add a daily increase of 10. We subtract 7 for daily wear and tear and we have a daily increase of 3 which is cumulative. In 10 days we have an increase of 30 which has raised the level to 130. We have a big fight which reduces the level by 50, leaving love at a low level of 80. However, the daily increase of 10 minus daily wear and tear of 7 continues . . . producing a true increase of 3 which is cumulative. After 7 days we have an increase of 3 times 7 which is 21. Added to the low level of 80 we have 101. Back to normal. (*He has written the following.*)

```
  100          10            7
 + 10          ×3           ×3
 ────         ────         ────
  110          30            21
                          
  − 7        +100          +80
 ────         ────         ────
  103          130           101
                          
              −50
             ────
               80
```

Here is the arithmetic of love. Ha! You think that is contradictory? Love and mathematics? Don't you know that you can take a yes and a no and push them together, squeeze them together, compress them so they are one? That in fact is what reality is? Opposites, contradictions compressed so that you don't know where one stops and the other begins? . . . Let us proceed.

(*He erases, and writes* On Hope.) And here is a picture of hope. (*He draws the following picture as he describes it.*)

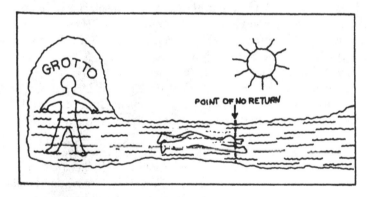

Man stands in his life, "Grotto." Always with a sense of being enclosed. He thinks of freedom, open space, air, sun. The only way out is always narrow, always arduous and frightening to cross. He dares. He fills his lungs with air. He swims. He is courageous. He reaches the point where, if he goes any further, he won't be able to return. "Point of no return." If he continues he might find the exit, if there is an exit . . . if the exit is within reach of his endurance. That is the point. Does he continue? Does he return? There is the picture of hope.

(*He erases and writes* On Cooking.) Have you ever cooked brussel sprouts? Miniature cabbage? Toy vegetable? Have you ever seen how beautiful they are?

(*He erases and writes* Summing Up.) And now, to conclude, I'll sing you a song.

The other day,
Looking at a weird-looking spider,
With legs ten times longer than its body,
Who moved in the most senseless and
Insane manner,
I said, "Spider, you are spastic and I am
A superior beast."

There! That is what it is all about.
Man is the rational animal

(*He exits.*)

END